GATEWAY TO THE QUANTUM AGE

Managing Disruptive Technologies In Globalized Knowledge Economies

Joseph Ponnoly

Gateway to the Quantum Age

Author: Joseph Ponnoly

Kindle Direct Publishing ISBN: 9781977050274

Published by: Cinfodens Consulting
Houston TX USA

Cover Page Photo:

"The Council", a ceramic sculpture by Bill Stewart, is displayed at the Rochester Airport, New York. Bill Stewart obtained his ideas from objects such as toys, games, and other artifacts salvaged by him.

The sculpture has relevance to the topic of the book - the emerging disruptive technologies of the quantum age, leading to the rise of AI, robotics, and super-intelligent machines and a new digital culture that is emerging. In the future, humans will have to confer, have council, with intelligent machines or will humans be just machines and 'smart fools'?

It also points to the need to merge art, science, and technology in the quantum age. Art and literature can help to steer humans in the right direction. The artwork also pinpoints the importance of creativity and innovation in the quantum digital age.

Technical advances must not lead to loss of the human touch. The question that arises is: are we stuck in the past or are we looking forward to an exciting future for humankind?

Photo by the author. 2017.

3

DEDICATION

Dedicated to *Rohit & Rohini*, my grandkids, who are always a source of my inspiration. Hope one day they will read this book and make their own improvements to its contents. Also dedicating this book to *Eliza*, my daughter, who always encouraged me to write, to my wife *Teresa*, who has been my life-partner for 39 years and to my son *Thejus*, who made me appreciate the joy of creation. Also dedicated to my mother *Aleykutty*, now aged 90, for her life-long sacrifices and dedication to her children, to my older brother *Johnnykutty* for his support, and to my father *Edoor Skaria Joseph* who left this earthly abode when I was less than two years old.

CONTENT

INTRODUCTION 12

LOOKING BACK 20

AN ODYSSEY --FROM VACUUM TUBES TO QUANTUM COMPUTERS --
A PERSONAL STORY.. 20
    IT in India 1975-2000 20
    The Post 2000 era in the USA 28

PART I 34

THE KNOWLEDGE ECONOMY IN AN INTERCONNECTEDWORLD 34

.... 35

THE KNOWLEDGE ECONOMY IN A QUANTUM WORLD 35
    The Digital Knowledge-Based Economy........................ 36
        The Flat World and the Lego World 37
        Knowledge-based Economy 38
        The Knowledge Society and the Knowledge Economy.......... 39
    The Evolution of the Information Age 40
        The evolution of the Internet 42
        Does IT Matter?.. 42
        Technology accelerators.................................. 44
        The Fourth Industrial Revolution......................... 45
        The Second Machine Age 46
    Crowdfunding 47
    AI and the Rise of the Robots................................ 48
    Platforms.. 51
    Exponential Organizations 55
        Uberization & Spotification 55
        Spotify.. 57
        Netflix 58
        AirbNb... 59
    Elon Musk, the architect of tomorrow........................ 60

The Big Five & the Challengers 62

    Facebook 62

    Amazon 64

    Apple 65

    Google 67

    Microsoft 67

    The Challengers 68

China, the digital frontier of the world 69

    The Chinese BAT 71

    Baidu 71

India's Digital Economy 73

Disruptive Technologies 75

The Evolution of Enterprise Technology 82

The Key Enablers 84

PART II 86

CORE TECHNOLOGIES 86

.... 87

WHITHER COMPUTING? 87

Super Computing 87

Quantum computing 89

    Quantum Bits (Qubits) 89

    Qubits and superposition 90

    Quantum entanglement 90

    Teleporting 91

    Computing power 92

    Current state of quantum computing 92

    Applications of quantum computing 94

Cloud Computing 95

    What is cloud computing? 97

    Virtualization 101

Edge Computing /Fog Computing 101

WAN Connectivity 102

    Digital Silk Road 102

Mobile & Communication Technologies 103

    5G 104

    Li-Fi vs. Wi-Fi 104

.... 106

THE SMART WORLD --INTERNET OF THINGS (IoT) 106

San Diego's Streetlight IoT Network 107

Object identification 109

Sensor Technology 110

Intelligent Network Infrastructure for IoT 111

    IoT Networks 113

IoT Data Analytics & Security 116

Smart Cities 116

    Futuristic Cities 118

    Challenges ahead for urban planning 120

Transportation 120

    Autonomous Vehicles 121

    Drones & Flying Taxis 122

LIVING WITH INTELLIGENT MACHINES 124

Artificial Intelligence 124

    Digital Virtual Assistants 126

    Robotic Soldiers 126

    Artificial Emotional Intelligence 127

    Robots That Feel 128

Robotics 129

    How do robots work? 132

    Industrial Robots 133

    Intelligent vs. Conscious Machines 134

    Robotic materials 135

    Space Robots 138

    Brain Computing – Controlling Machines by Thought 139

    Cognitive Computing & Neuro Science 141

HARNESSING THE POWER OF BIG DATA 143

Data as Knowledge Source 144

From Business Intelligence to Data Analytics 145

Business Intelligence 145

Evolution of Data Analytics.................................. 146

Challenges of big data 146

Analytical competition.. 147

Big Data 148

Unstructured data 149

MapReduce, Hadoop & Spark 150

Data Science.. 151

Big Data Analytics 151

Analytics Software 153

Big Data Injection Tools for IoT Sensor Data - Microsoft...... 153

Data Analytics using Amazon Web Services (AWS) 154

Predictive Analytics & Data Mining.......................... 156

Insight into Data 157

Machine Learning & Machine Intelligence 157

Content and Text Analytics.................................. 158

Why predictions fail?.. 159

Data-driven decision making 159

Data Management & Storage 160

Data Availability... 160

Trusting data.. 161

Security Requirements of Big Data........................ 161

Data Confidentiality & Privacy............................. 162

The barriers 162

Big Data in Practice 163

The Dark Side of Big Data...................................... 166

Wisdom lies in Small Data...................................... 167

IN CODE WE TRUST --THE ALGORITHMIC WORLD 168

MACHINE LEARNING 169

Machine Learning Algorithms 170

Unsupervised Learning techniques - Clustering 171

Supervised Learning 171

Support Vector Machines..................................... 172

Random Forests.. 172

Applications of Machine Learning methods 173

Reinforcement Learning 173

Importance of training data and feature selection for predictive accuracy 174

Feature extraction 175

Data Mining Algorithms 175

Neural Networks.. 177

Clustering methods 178

Logistical Regression... 178

Machine Learning Tools 179

SOFTWARE ENGINEERING... 180

Structured Systems Analysis & Design (SSAD).................... 181

Agile Methodology 182

DevOps approach 183

Architectural Approach 186

Monolith vs. MicoServices Architecture........................ 186

The World of APIs & Digital Platforms 187

RESTful API... 188

Can we trust code? 190

PART III 191

APPLIED TECH 191

.... 192

THE FUTURE OF MANUFACTURING 192

Robotic Manufacturing 193

Manufacturers of Industrial Robots 194

Collaborative robots 195

3D Printing and Additive Manufacturing 196

Nanotechnologies... 198

Applications of Additive Manufacturing........................ 199

DIGITAL BANKING, FIN-TECH AND DIGITAL TRUST................... 202

Digital Trust.. 203

Blockchain Technology.. 204

Cryptography – the power behind block chain technology.. 205

Blockchain technology applications for digital trust 209

Private Blockchains..213

ConsenSys and DAOs for value creation..............214

Creating a Smart Contract 214

Limitations of blockchains 215

Crypto Currencies 215

Creating your Bitcoin wallet 221

Mobile Payment Systems..225

GENERAL APPLICATION AREAS..................................227

Virtual Reality & Augmented Reality (Immersive Computing) . 228

Augmented Reality (AR) 229

VR and AR for workplace collaboration...............230

Mixed Reality 231

Industrial Augmented Reality 231

Vision for the Visually Impaired.........................232

Virtual World of Simulations 232

Social Media & Instant Messaging 233

Entertainment...234

Medicine and Healthcare.......................................234

Bio-printing..236

Bio-Technology 237

Gene Editing –CRISPR/Cas9 --the power to control evolution
....237

Gene Modified vs. Gene edited Crops.................239

Transforming Education through MOOCs.................240

Agriculture & Healthy Eating 242

Food Computing – the New Green Revolution.......243

Hydroponic Cultivation.....................................244

Vertical Farming 244

PART IV 246

THE FUTURE OF TECHNOLOGY & 246

RISKS 246

LOOKING INTO THE CRYSTAL BALL 247

How Far is Singularity? 250
Dealing with cyberspace risks 252
    Cybercrimes 253
    Digital Identity 253
    Privacy 254
    Safe Computing 256
    Technology Addiction 256
    Cyber Security 257
    Dealing with Fake News in the Age of Untruth 260
    Risk Management 260
Cyberwar 261
    Cyber Peace Keepers 262
Technology for Humans 263
    Humanized technology 264
Food for Thought 268

REFERENCES 270

ACKNOWLEDGMENTS 277

ABOUT THE AUTHOR 279

Gateway to the Quantum Age 281

INTRODUCTION

Welcome to our quantum future.

Much of our life today is digital. It is being defined by smart technologies powered by global internet connectivity. Computer systems, networks, data processing systems, and information systems have become an integral part of business and organizations, and even everyday life.

Looking back, the ideas of information revolution and digital age have been around since the 1960s. Almost six decades later, we are feeling their impact more than ever. Every aspect of human life is now impacted by digital technologies, whether it is by the smart phone, tablet or the notebook, or smart devices monitoring health, securing homes, or controlling traffic. Information is everywhere at the press of a button.

Technology today is making sweeping changes in the world in all spheres. Our future as individuals and the future of corporations and organizations, of societies, and nations, are going to be increasingly driven by new and disruptive technologies. We are now leapfrogging into a quantum world and quantum age, where we must compete with intelligent machines, and even co-exist with them.

With quantum computing on the horizon, we can call the coming era the quantum age. Quantum processing will radically change the way information is processed and may lead to cure for cancer or may help to solve the climate change, as pointed out by Satya Nadella, CEO of Microsoft. Adoption of quantum physics into information processing will lead to processing power and speeds far superior to what we have today.

New digital technologies such as quantum computing, artificial intelligence and robotics, cloud computing, IoT (Internet of Things), 3D Printing, blockchain, cryptocurrency, big data analytics, virtual reality, augmented reality, autonomous vehicles, sensor technologies, etc. are emerging, and they are transforming organizations and human lives in more radical ways than ever before.

We are also in a new age of automation, where robots are fast replacing manual laborers on the shop floor and even in the services sector. They are also replacing truck drivers, and even skilled professionals such as lawyers, nurses, and physicians.

We are seeing a new awakening and the emergence of a new digital culture. A digital renaissance is in the offing.

Managing disruptive technologies

What are the emerging technologies that will disrupt the knowledge-based economy? What are the barriers to organizational effectiveness in this digitally networked world where knowledge is easily available, but knowledge-management is difficult? How do we promote and manage innovation? How do we manage knowledge-workers, and the intellectual capital of organizations?

INTRODUCTION

How do organizations redeploy the labor being displaced by robots and intelligent machines?

Managing knowledge and data

Information is the lifeblood of organizations. Today, technology drives information and knowledge. How can we manage technology and derive value and competitive edge by leveraging information technology and operational technology? How do we determine which emerging technologies are suitable for an organization? How do we manage new and disruptive technologies?

In the knowledge economy, the focus has shifted from just information to knowledge and knowledge-workers and their intellectual capital, creativity, and ability to innovate. The emphasis has also shifted to knowledge derived from data and information, and on data analytics.

Digital Transformation and Digital Leadership

The rapid pace of technological change is calling for transformation of business and organizations in a radical and revolutionary manner. Managing the digital transformation is a major challenge. It involves rethinking business models and strategies. New organizational structures are to be in place. Managing the transformational change requires visionary and strong leadership.

What does this book cover?

This book tries to give an overview of the quantum age,

the knowledge-based economy and emerging digital technology landscape, the technologies that disrupt every business, industry, geography, and human life today.

It also discusses the key drivers and enablers of the knowledge economy and the quantum age in addition to the disruptive technologies --the people and their innovative minds, the knowledge that is derived from massive volumes of data, the algorithms that help to derive knowledge from data, and the systems that are built or disrupted, leading to the creation and sustenance of the knowledge economy and the emerging digital culture.

The book also points out the challenges of managing technology and the emerging cyberspace risks and threats.

Topics covered are:

Quantum computing, cloud computing, edge computing, mobile and communication technologies.

The Smart World: Internet of Things (IoT), Sensor Technologies, Autonomous Vehicles

Artificial Intelligence, Robotics & Machine Learning, Brain computing

3D Printing and digital manufacturing

Digital banking and Fin-Tech driven by blockchain technology and crypto currencies

Virtual Reality, Augmented Reality, Social Media, Entertainment, Medicine & Healthcare, Wearables, online education MOOCs, Food computing

INTRODUCTION

Big Data Analytics

Machine Learning Algorithms & The Algorithmic World

I have been a witness to the evolution of the knowledge economy during the past four decades. I have also been an active participant to a certain extent in adoption or evangelizing many of these technologies, in India and in the USA. The first part of the book titled 'an odyssey – from vacuum tubes to quantum computers' gives a brief overview of my journey through the digital age.

The target audience

The book is meant for anyone who wants to be aware of 1) the emerging disruptive technologies that will drive the future of organizations, and 2) the drivers and enablers of the emerging knowledge economy and society.

The book is intended to help business leaders and managers understand the broad implications of emerging digital technologies, to help them embrace the technologies that they need, and to help them spearhead digital transformations required within their sphere of activity, to harness the power of data and algorithms, and to create innovative systems using the intellectual capital of humans.

The book is also targeted at technologists and innovators to help them understand the broad social and economic impact of the technologies that they create or implement, so that they can provide value to customers and stakeholders and help advance the knowledge economy and knowledge society.

Leaders, managers, and technologists must facilitate and drive the evolution of a humanized digital culture and create a better future for humankind.

Students of management and computer information systems, and even students of philosophy, could use this book to supplement their classroom classes on topics related to management information systems, digital / knowledge economy, technology management, digital leadership, disruptive technologies, knowledge society, and digital culture.

How this book is organized

The chapters are grouped into four parts:

- Part I: Knowledge Economy
- Part II: Core Technologies
- Part III: Applied Technologies
- Part IV: The Future of Technology & Risks

The various parts or chapters do not follow any sequential order. The readers can choose any section to read in any order that they feel like.

INTRODUCTION

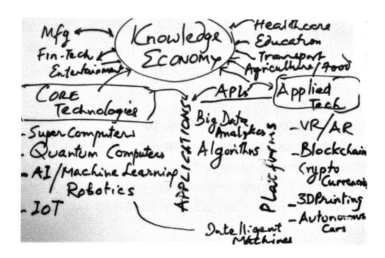

PART I: EMERGING DIGITAL BUSINESS & KNOWLEDGE ECONOMY IN AN INTERCONNECTED WORLD

Part I deals with the knowledge-based economy that is evolving and the players in the field

PART II: CORE TECHNOLOGIES OF THE QUANTUM AGE

Part II gives an overview of the core technologies:

Quantum computing, cloud computing, edge computing, mobile and communication technologies.

Internet of Things (IoT), sensor technologies, smart world, autonomous vehicles

Artificial Intelligence, Robotics & Machine Learning, Brain computing

Big Data Analytics

The Algorithms & Applications

PART III: APPLIED TECHNOLOGIES

3D Printing and digital manufacturing

Digital banking and Fin-Tech driven by blockchain technology and crypto currencies

General Application areas such as Virtual Reality, Augmented Reality, Social Media, Healthcare & Medicine, Wearables, online education MOOCs, Food computing

PART IV: FUTURE OF TECHNOLOGY & RISKS

This section also points to the challenges of managing technology and deals with the emerging cyberspace risks and threats.

If this book helps you to think about and view this digital world differently, the purpose is served. I will appreciate your comments and feedback.

Joseph Ponnoly

Chapter 1

LOOKING BACK

AN ODYSSEY --FROM VACUUM TUBES TO QUANTUM COMPUTERS -- A PERSONAL STORY

IT in India 1975-2000

It has been a journey for over four decades. This is my personal story -- my encounter with electronics and computing, from vacuum tubes and punched cards to big data analytics, artificial intelligence, and quantum computing. It is intended to put in perspective the rapid technological advancements and innovations and the exponential growth of technology that we are experiencing today.

During the 1973-75 period in Kerala (India), when I was pursuing my Masters degree in Physics with concentration in Electronics, we conducted experiments using cathode ray tubes and vacuum tubes, and built radios using transistors. We then learnt Boolean algebra and the theory of logic circuits that are at the heart of today's digital computer processors and memory. We did not then learn about integrated circuits or microprocessors, though LSI chips appeared in 1969 and the Intel 4004 microprocessor had hit the market in 1971. Computing technology was much developed in USA ever since the development of the ENIAC in 1946. Particularly since the 1960s, computers were used in NASA mission control and Apollo missions. However, many of us, even students of electronics in India, were hardly aware of those developments, as these topics did not find mention in our syllabus. We did have a seminar on digital computers. It piqued my interest in computing.

My interest in electronics and emerging digital computing technology continued as a hobby, even after my joining CBI (Central Bureau of Investigation- India) pursuing a career in crime investigation. I passed out of SVP National Police Academy in 1976, having studied criminal law, forensic science & forensic medicine, investigation and police science, criminology, and allied subjects. While in the police academy, I wrote an article in the academy journal on computers for the police and I found that then India had only around 270 computers. The main ones were used in Indian Institute of Science, Bangalore, Indian Statistical Institute, Indian Institutes of Technology, Indian Meteorological Department, in some of the research institutes of the Government of India, and some of the public-sector institutes and banks and in some university centers. Most of the computers were IBM 360/370 or ICL mainframe computers or mini-computers PDP 11 from Digital Equipment. The Electronics Corporation of India (ECIL), Hyderabad (established in 1967) was manufacturing TDC 312 and 316 computers and they were

21

called 'mainframe computers'. All these computers were based on punched card inputs and they were to be programmed using COBOL, FORTRAN or PL/1 and later BASIC languages. In the Indian police, only the Border Security Force had a computer (ECIL TDC 316), and it was used mainly for payroll processing.

In early 1982, while working in CBI Madras (Chennai), on my own, I enrolled in a one-year computer programming course that was offered by Annamalai University in distance education mode. The course covered COBOL, FORTRAN, PL/1, and BASIC programming. Lab exercises were performed on the TDC 316 mainframe computer on campus at Annamalai University. Immediately after completing that course, I enrolled for a course on Computer Software & Applications at NIIT Madras, when NIIT started their center in Madras (Chennai). It was offered as a part-time course that would not interfere with my official work. The course followed the curriculum of Carnegie Mellon University. The structured systems analysis and design projects and COBOL programming projects gave me enough hands-on experience in developing information systems. It must be mentioned that I was discouraged from continuing these studies by my boss, indicating how police officers then did not see any use of technology in police work. But since I was doing it in my spare time spending money from my own pocket, he could not prevent me from pursuing my interests, as I could not be faulted on any count on my investigations. For me every crime investigation also was like solving a puzzle.

During early 1980s, National Informatics Center set up by

Government of India had started computerizing information systems in all central government departments. For development of crime management information systems in CBI, my knowledge of systems analysis and design and programming became useful and I was able to suggest design of various input forms and input data codification, processing logic, and report formats.

It was during this period that we started investigating against a major firm that started offering PCs manufactured in India. The investigation covered unauthorized imports and customs duty violations. The firm was importing the various PC components including the microprocessors, motherboard, memory chips, storage disks, and then assembling them and selling them as Indian-made PCs. The PC components were imported mostly from Singapore through agents declaring them differently as articles that were authorized for import and at reduced customs duty. This case further piqued my interest in emerging technologies.

During 1985 or so, I was investigating a major fraud case in Archaeological Survey of India. With tens of thousands of transactions involving daily muster-rolls (labor attendance) and inventory and purchase of items for maintenance of an 11th century Chola temple, it would have been quite difficult to prove that the records were manipulated. Anyone visiting the temple would know its true state after seeing the dilapidated condition of the temple. In the name of maintenance, Rs.20 to Rs.25 lakhs would be shown spent for labor and materials, and the relevant records would be cooked up. How to prove that these records were manipulated, was the question. In the

normal course, using manual processing, it would have
been difficult to comb through a room full of these records
stacked from floor to ceiling. I would have been justified
in spending time for investigation for over a year and then
closing the case for want of sufficient evidence. It was then
that I thought of using my computer skills. I hired
computer time, used a PC and database (then Dbase-2) and
created simple database records and sorted them in various
ways. This is not different from any of the current data
analytics applications for fraud detection. Without going
into details, it was easy for me to identify the fraudulent
entries, the forged signatures or thumb impressions on the
labor records and finish the investigation successfully in
four months. Smt Letika Saran IPS, then SP, CBI, Madras
gave me support and encouragement.

My use of computers later became sporadic, as CBI was
not in need of such expertise then. However, in 1988
during the investigation of a disproportionate assets case
against an IAS Officer, I was able to use computers for
compiling financial data to re-create the personal balance
sheet and income, expenditure, assets statements of the
IAS officer over several years based on data from various
sources. Most of the financial transactions had to be
reconstructed.

During 1990, I got transferred to the Computer Center of
the CBI in New Delhi, on my request. NIC had already
developed a Crime Information System using Foxbase in a
XENIX networked environment. During the next eight
years, I got the opportunity to work with an external
consultant MecSpert Systems run by Madhava Challa and
S Seri Reddy. I also worked with teams from NIC and

CMC Limited thanks to the guidance and supervision of Dr. K. Subramanian and G. Sudeswaran of NIC, to computerize and network all the branches of CBI and to help establish the dedicated connectivity with the global Interpol network. During this period, we developed systems and applications to aid crime investigations, ventured into computer crime investigations and forensics, searches and seizures in digital environments, collection of digital evidence, and developed a computer-based crime and criminal intelligence system, in addition to Management Information Systems. I must give due credit to the brilliant and committed teams that we had.

My earlier use of computers to aid crime investigations got acknowledged. I was attached to the Rajiv Gandhi Assassination case team. The encouragement, support, and total independence that I was given by my bosses during those eight years helped me and my great teams to develop an evidence analysis system, an event sequential analysis system for crime reconstruction, a communication analysis system for identifying networks of organized criminals including terrorists. The idea for compiling and analyzing the massive amount of data collected on crime and criminals, led to starting a new unit for criminal intelligence. These tools were effectively used in a number of sensational cases such as the Harshad Mehta cases (involving the Mumbai stock market scam), Punjab Chief Minister Beant Singh's Assassination case, and the Bombay Blasts of 1993 involving the Bombay underworld.

It was during this period that the need arose for developing expertise to collect digital evidence from computers and computer networks. The Jain Hawala case was a case in point. This gave birth to computer forensics in India. The emergence of computer viruses transferred via floppy disks forced us to think of computer and information security and to develop expertise in that field too.

A new area that emerged was the field of computer-based crimes and computer frauds. Computer crime investigation became a new area requiring new investigation capabilities. The first computer fraud that was investigated by CBI was the NDMC (New Delhi Municipal Corporation) billing fraud. The IIT engineer who developed the COBOL program for billing was managing the systems, LAN network, and managing the data in file systems. He could easily manipulate the billing data for bank remittance and misappropriate the collections that were excluded from bank remittance. Since the reconciliations and audit took months, he could easily get away without being detected. Finally the long arm of the law fell on him.

It was during 1995-96 that I got involved in the Purulia Arms Drop Case. The case was unearthed by decoding the contents of a notebook computer that was obtained from the chartered plane that was used to airdrop large cache of arms of ammunition in Purulia, W.Bengal. The files were erased, and the hard-disk was formatted, though this was not obvious to the computer engineers who first examined the notebook in Bombay (Mumbai). This was the first case in India where digital evidence was admitted in an Indian court.

In 1996, I was deputed as part of a two-member team to represent India at the 2nd International Conference on Computer Crimes that was held by Interpol at the Interpol

Headquarters in Lyon, France. It was in this conference that a global strategy was discussed and developed to deal with computer crimes globally. On our return we gave recommendations to the Government of India 1) to enact legislation to deal with computer crimes; 2) to set up dedicated computer crime investigation and forensics units at the central and state level in India; 3) to train police officers on IT, computer crimes, computer crime investigations and computer forensics. As a result, India finally enacted the IT Act in 2000. At the CBI level, we started training courses for police officers in CBI Academy. Dedicated cybercrime investigation and forensics units were set up in CBI and State Police agencies in due course.

In 1998 I opted for voluntary retirement from CBI, deciding to focus only on IT as a career. I started my own software consulting company in New Delhi, in partnership with the late Wg. Cdr. K.P.Srinivasan. We developed software for various PSUs (Public Sector Undertakings) and also conducted IT and information security training courses in various metros in India. Shri Neeraj Kumar IPS, and Shri R.N.Kaul, Jt Director, CBI, continued to engage me in CBI projects and I continued to teach in the CBI Academy designing courses in IT Security. Shri A.P.Singh IPS, then CVO of Indian Airlines (later Director, CBI) engaged me as his consultant during this period. Following this we were able to develop systems in a few PSUs in India and conduct IT awareness and security seminars in several metros in India.

The Post 2000 era in the USA

In 2000, I migrated to the US. Since then I have focused mostly on information security having worked with a software development company and various MNCs in the banking and financial services, healthcare, technology, and manufacturing sectors. There were many challenges in helping organizations to manage systems and technology, risks of technology and information, and regulatory compliance. These involved legacy systems as well as cutting-edge technologies. During this period, I was able to experience the dot-com bust, and the quantum leap in technology since the early 2000s. The disruptions in technology, business, and the global economy, required continuous updating of skills and knowledge.

The topics in this book will be more related to the Post 2000 era when e-commerce companies having ruled the roost since the late 1990s suddenly fell, and then rose again like a phoenix. Since then we have seen the exponential growth of disruptive technologies.

My first project in USA was in a dot-com healthcare company in New Jersey, for developing an e-prescription (electronic prescription) system to enable physicians to use a PDA (Personal Digital Assistant) a Palm Pilot, to record diagnosis notes and corresponding procedures based on the diagnosis and procedure codes, and then make drug prescriptions based on various parameters—the insurance coverage, drug-to-drug interactions, etc. The prescribed drug information is to be beamed securely over the cellular network to a web server, which then transfers the information to the concerned drug store over the web so that the patient can pick up the drugs at the drug store. Payment is also to be authorized online by the health insurance company.

The dot-com bust of 2000 brought down major e-commerce companies because of lack of web security. The ecommerce market fell, and my client company also did not weather the storm, though the project was completed, went live, and physicians and pharmacies started using the application.

My sponsor based in Michigan then ventured into development of software to implement HIPAA EDI standards for health care transactions including payments. A new company was formed to create a web portal to enable HIPAA EDI transactions. Rupesh Srivastava, CEO, and Sandeep Upadhyaya, VP, were entrepreneurs with a vision and passion. We also developed expertise to comply with HIPAA security and privacy standards and organized and delivered corporate training on HIPAA-related standards.

Since information security became an important focus area, I got certified as a CISSP (Certified Information Systems Security Professional) and CISA (Certified Information Systems Auditor) in 2001. I then joined a major financial services company in Columbus, OH. During the next six years I focused on risk assessments and regulatory compliance, and all aspects of information security including networks, applications, systems and data protection, in a major banking and financial services company. It brought me face to face with legacy mainframe systems technologies as well as the state-of-the art technologies. The company was an IBM Center of Excellence for computing. It was also one of the first companies to use grid computing for actuarial processing that required super computing power for the required calculations to determine insurance premium. Grid computing used the unused processing power of networked computers at any point in time, to provide supercomputing processing power, to perform computing intensive applications. It was challenging to perform risk assessments for nearly hundred projects every year covering various aspects of business and technology in multi-billion-dollar business segments including banking.

During this period, I had the privilege to work with some of the best technologists, managers, leaders, and business brains. Jack Jones, who was CISO, became a role-model. The FAIR risk assessment methodology, now globally accepted, was developed by Jack Jones during this period, and we were the guinea pigs. Working with several professionals such as Dan Houser, Bill Cox, Mark Chamberlain, and John Rockwood was an education by itself. My association with ISACA and ISSA Chapters helped me to hone up my knowledge and skills in IT, information security and IS auditing. During this period, I also completed my MBA from Ashland University with concentration in Finance and investments.

I also enrolled for a Ph.D. program in computer information systems at Nova Southeastern University (NSU), Fort Lauderdale, Florida. After six years into the Ph.D. program, I had to drop out at the dissertation stage, as my studies were interfering with my professional career. My dissertation was on phishing detection using machine learning techniques. The doctoral studies helped me to come to grips with state-of-the-art technology including machine learning and artificial intelligence, knowledge engineering, aspect-oriented programming, privacy-enhancing-technologies, and cryptography.

To cope up with my doctoral studies, I joined a consulting company, a spin-off of Deloitte. While working with this consulting company, I worked for a major healthcare company and a major technology company. The work in both these companies were mostly focused on internal controls and regulatory compliance including SOX (Sarbanes-Oxley Act) and PCI.

Next, I worked with a major manufacturing company in Ohio. This was more challenging, as the systems and networks were all outsourced and managed by EDS (later acquired by HP). We had to implement information security best practices conforming to ISO 27000 standards in an SAP ERP environment and had to implement identity and access control systems to interface with SAP systems, web portal, exchange server, and Active Directory. This was quite challenging. Computer forensics and eDiscovery systems using EnCase had also to be implemented.

For the next four years I was engaged with a major healthcare company involved in cancer care and research in Houston TX. I had to deal with risk assessments for major projects involving various technologies, applications, and interfaces, and had to implement systems for vulnerability and threat management. I also had to deal with advanced tools, as also processes, and had to train system administrators. As a premier research center in the world, it employed the best technologies. IBM Watson technology was implemented by the Institute to identify genomic patterns related to various cancers. It was ground breaking research. I worked with some of the best professionals, researchers, and technologists there.

My next major engagement was with a major global investment bank in Manhattan, New York. This was challenging since a lot of coordination was required between the headquarters in Germany and the Regional Office in New York. It involved reviewing the internal control systems, standardizing them to conform to COBIT & ISO Standards, implementing required systems and creating an automated workflow for internal review of the implementation and functioning of the controls for certification by senior management.

Next major engagement was with a major manufacturing company in New York. This involved a number of projects: implementing EnCase for eDiscovery and Computer Forensics Investigations, architecting security for implementation of 3D Printing for manufacturing, real-time security monitoring implementation of global manufacturing systems, cloud computing data broker and OAuth (authentication) implementation, SSO (Single Sign-On) implementation for financial reporting, VPN connectivity for a robotic manufacturing system, risk management and controls for global payroll implementation, metadata-based access control for research documents and intellectual property. It was interesting to see how a global company in the forefront of nanotechnology research was trying to protect its intellectual property.

That was my journey from the vacuum tube era to the current quantum computing age. My experience can be summed up in two words: problem solving. In my view, computing (as also criminal investigation) is all about problem solving and innovation. The journey continues.

Against this backdrop, the following pages contain my perception of how emerging technologies are shaping a quantum world.

PART I
THE KNOWLEDGE ECONOMY IN AN INTERCONNECTEDWO RLD

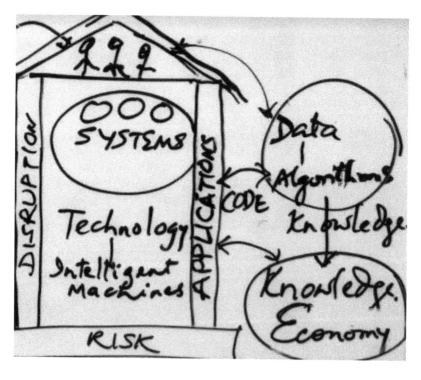

Chapter 2

THE KNOWLEDGE ECONOMY IN A QUANTUM WORLD

"In the twenty-first century, businesses exist in a Lego world"

-Elizabeth Haas Edersheim, in *'The Definitive Drucker'*

Businesses and organizations today function in a global environment, engaging diverse global workforce or intellectual capital. Technology today drives business, instead of just supporting or enabling it. Communication today is instantaneous at the speed of light. Information and communication technologies have helped to evolve a global digital economy that is knowledge-based. Intelligent machines that are being developed, have self-learning capabilities, replacing humans in many areas such as in factories, in the battle-field, and even in the service sector.

With the emergence of quantum computing, processing power of computers is increasing at a tremendous pace, helping humans to solve highly complex problems with the help of intelligent and more powerful data-crunching machines. A new era driven by machine learning, artificial intelligence, and robotics is evolving where humans and intelligent machines must co-exist and work side by side.

Since the 1960s, for nearly five decades, the world has seen the impact, beneficial or otherwise, of the digital revolution. The development of the personal computer in the 1980s, the Internet disrupting the world in the mid-1990s, the rise of ecommerce, were all factors that ushered in a global digital economy. With the adoption of cloud computing, mobile and smart phone technologies, connected devices and Internet of Everything, and quantum computing on the horizon, our lives are changing fast. Social media today disseminates information across the globe within seconds. It is a powerful media for social intelligence and social consciousness. These rapid technological advances are impacting businesses, organizations, societies, and individuals globally.

The Digital Knowledge-Based Economy

Towards the latter part of the 1990s, the Internet (the network of networks) was thrown open to the public and the world, from what was then a safely guarded secret technology of the ARPA (Advanced Research Projects Agency) of the US Government. Don Tapscott in his book 'The Digital Economy' (1995) referred to the then emerging internetworked business as the main characteristic of the digital economy that was then emerging. He underlined the impact of the Internet on businesses globally. The Internet is today the backbone of the knowledge economy, where knowledge is the engine driving the economy in the world.

The Flat World and the Lego World

The Internet, powered by advances in computing and communication technologies, has led to globalization and a flattened world, as noted by Thomas L Friedman, New York Times columnist, and author of the book *'The World is Flat'* (2005). He refers to the world as flat or easily accessible without physical or national boundaries, because of the enabling of speedy communication and collaboration on a global scale. Globalization has been an equalizing force, creating a flattened global playing field, and providing unprecedented economic opportunities. He details the forces that led to Business Process Outsourcing (BPO), resulting in China and India emerging as the global centers for manufacturing and IT services respectively. The globally connected flattened world provides multiple forms of collaboration. For businesses to cope up in this flat world, they have to consolidate, and provide new value to their customers. According to Friedman, it did not matter where in the world the work got done, because communication transcends time and space.

As pointed out by Elizabeth Haas Edersheim, in '*The Definitive Drucker*' (2017), Peter F Drucker would disagree with Friedman as Friedman considered only the two dimensions of space and time to point out the far-reaching impact of globalization of business. Drucker would point out that barriers exist for business even in the same geographical region, or industry.

According to Drucker, in the twenty-first century businesses exist in a Lego world. Legos represent not just software and components, but people and their knowledge and expertise existing within the enterprise and outside.

They need to be connected through innovative approaches. Businesses must put together Lego pieces from various sources to complete the picture of their vision and mission. An American company's Legos in manufacturing, supply chain, distribution, expertise, or services may have to connect with related Legos in Sweden or South Africa. This globalized Lego network will characterize twenty-first century business. No business is an island and no part of business can exist in isolation or silos. It is a Lego world in business.

As mentioned by Edersheim, the Lego approach to disconnect and reconnect Legos as required is followed by Dell and Amazon, to provide innovative solutions and products.

Knowledge-based Economy

In the 1960s, main-frame computers from IBM and mini computers from Digital Equipment promoted automation of business processes. The development of computing technologies and the emergence of automated information processing replaced manual record keeping. Manufacturing also saw the benefits of automation replacing manual labor. This led to development of knowledge technologies focused on information processing and resulting knowledge driving various sectors of the economy.

The emergence of the knowledge economy saw the dominance of the service sector as against the manufacturing sector of earlier decades. In 1969, Peter Drucker in his book *The Age of Discontinuity* referred to what he then saw as the disruptive and radical changes and discontinuity in the economy, polity, and society, resulting from adoption of knowledge technologies managed by knowledge workers. He foresaw then that these disruptive changes were leading to transformation of the global economic landscape and leading to the emergence of a knowledge-based economy and society globally.

The major areas of discontinuity he referred to were:

- Knowledge technologies or computer-based information technology
- The change from a national and international economy to a world economy
- Social changes and transformation of society with an evolving society of organizations

The Knowledge Society and the Knowledge Economy

In a knowledge economy, the knowledge workers (professional, managerial, and technical people) replace the manual labor, and academic knowledge replaces the experience gained over decades by people doing repetitive jobs, whether manual or administrative.

Today, as predicted by Prof Drucker, knowledge industries based on ideas and information are rapidly replacing industries supplying goods and services, particularly in developed economies, with ramifications across the globe.

According to Drucker, businesses selling products and services are disappearing. Today businesses are selling experience. Competition is also disappearing. A solutions market is emerging. Those who sell better solutions survive, and others will die. Businesses must have a shared vision, and must promote innovation and productivity, to have a cutting edge in the emerging solutions market.

The Evolution of the Information Age

Before diving deep into the emerging technologies, let us look at the impact of technology on business during the past five decades of the information age. Today technology has become a business enabler and business driver. Operations Technology is part and parcel of manufacturing and industrial operations. Robotic systems have replaced manual labor in many industrial operations and even in surgical operations. Similarly, Information Technology is now an integral part of business, supporting business decision making. Relevant and quality information that is available in real-time and when required at various levels, would make organizations more efficient and effective.

A few areas where information is crucial for business operations can be mentioned, though the type of information and intelligence required may vary from industry to industry, or from organization to organization. Businesses need marketing and sales information, customer information, information on customer complaints and feedback, information on financial status, income, expenditures, tax and costs, budget and performance variance, stock performance information, banking and debt information, information on employee engagement, turnover, recruitment, training, information on technical resources, facilities, safety, production, inventory, supply chain information, operational information, information on systems –hardware, software, databases, access, risks, information on compliance, audit, and management information and intelligence, through data analytics.

From the 1960s through the 1970s of the mainframe era and particularly since the 1980s of the PC age, organizations have been on the technology bandwagon. Computer-based information technology has been widely adopted in organizations globally for the past fifty years for commercial and business applications. Organizations since then have made huge investments in information and communications technologies. The old manual filing and paper-based systems are today obsolete and are replaced by digital systems and electronically stored data. With networking technologies and personal computers entering the market in the 1980s, access to information became easier from a desktop computer. Email and instant messaging communications have led to faster access to information for increased productivity and collaboration at various levels in an organization.

In the July 1985 issue of Harvard Business Review, *Prof Michael E. Porter and Victor E. Millar* analyzed in detail how information and information technology give business and organizations a competitive advantage. They pointed out that the information revolution was sweeping through the economy and that no company could escape its effects. A company's value chain is a system of interdependent activities and includes inbound logistics, operations, outbound logistics, marketing and sales along with the support activities such as infrastructure, human resource management, technology development and procurement. They analyzed how IT could improve productivity and reduce costs in every phase of the value chain, thus transforming the value chain.

The evolution of the Internet

It was in 1989 that the British Engineer Tim Berners-Lee
invented the World Wide Web (WWW), building on
hypertext and hypertext markup language (html) links to
create online documents. With the US Telecom Act, 1996,
the Internet became unregulated and was released from the
controls of DARPA (Defense Advanced Research Projects
Agency of US Government). Developments in
communications technology helped to evolve the web and
online media globally to spread information and digital
content and for social communications through email
systems, and later through instant messaging systems, and
social media. E-journals and blogs were part of this
evolution.

The Internet revolution of the mid 1990s made
information accessible over the web. Online or dot-com
companies and e-commerce mushroomed.

Does IT Matter?

And then there was the dot-com bust in 2000. Many of
the e-commerce companies were wiped out. The larger
corporate companies that invested heavily in information
technology did not see adequate returns on investment.
The seminal paper and book of by Prof Nicholas G. Carr
titled '*Does IT matter?*' (2004) pointed to the great IT
debacle. He expressed the sentiments of organizations on
the wasted information technology investments and the
vanishing advantage. Questions arose as to what the role
of technology in organizations is and how to leverage

technology for competitive advantage. The book pointed out urgent need for Governance and Management of IT and IT investments.

What many organizations did in computerization projects was to invest heavily to keep up with the Joneses. The problem was not in the technologies. The problem was in failing to perform adequate systems analysis for requirements gathering and in systems design and implementation, maintenance, and monitoring, in not aligning technology strategies (assuming they existed) with business strategies and in not taking an architectural approach to systems development, implementation and maintenance. Problems also arose in not considering technology risks and in not implementing information security safeguards or controls to protect sensitive data, web applications, systems, networks and communication channels. Identity and access control mechanisms were not given adequate attention. Even where systems and data were breached, incident management mechanisms were absent. Business continuity and disaster recovery systems were also not given adequate importance.

Steve Case who was one of the pioneers of Internet Technology in the 1990s, in his book *'The Third Wave of the Internet'* (2016) analyzes the rise and use of the Internet since 1985. His concept is similar to Alvin Toffler's *'Third Wave'* published in 1980. Toffler's wave theory focused on how human society was radically transformed by agriculture, industrial revolution and the information age. Toffler published *'Power Shift'* in 1990 and *'Revolutionary Wealth'* in 2006 expanding on this 'Third Wave' concept.

THE KNOWLEDGE ECONOMY IN A QUANTUM WORLD

Steve Case explains that the 1985-1999 period saw the first wave of computerization, networking and use of the Internet and the rapid adoption of e-commerce by companies in the 1990s. The second wave during the period 2000-2015 stabilized e-commerce with the shifting focus on secure web computing. According to him 2016 has seen the dawn of the Third Wave of the Internet with interconnected devices and the Internet of Everything.

Technology accelerators

Prof Jim Collins in his book *'Good to Great'* mentions how great companies have been pioneers in use of technology for competitive advantage. These companies used different technologies depending on their requirements. For example, Kroger pioneered the use of bar-code technology to scan products and to improve inventory management. Gillette used automated manufacturing technologies. Chrysler and Ford used computer-aided design. Today Amazon heavily uses robotic systems in their fulfillment centers. Many companies such as GE and Capital One are now adopting cloud-based systems taking advantage of security, financial and operational advantages of cloud computing offered by Amazon Web Services, Microsoft Azure, IBM, Google and other reputed cloud service providers providing various cloud services – Infrastructure, Platforms and Systems or Applications as a service—similar to utility services such as electricity.

Instead of having in-house data-centers and systems that are hard to maintain, organizations are migrating their computing requirements to these cloud service providers.

The question remains as to what technologies to adopt and

how much of technology to use and invest in, while managing the huge operational expenditures for maintaining legacy systems and technologies.

The Fourth Industrial Revolution

Prof. Klaus Schwab, Economist and Founder Chairman of World Economic Forum, in his book *The Fourth Industrial Revolution*' (2016) points to the rapid technological, social and economic transformation taking place in society globally because of emerging technologies.

He feels that human society globally is going through a fourth industrial revolution, considering the exponential speed of social transformation, the breadth and depth of digital technologies, and their impact on systems across companies, countries, industries, and societies. The change is fundamental and global.

The agrarian revolution that happened 10,000 years ago resulted in domestication of animals, increased food production, and gave rise to larger human settlements, leading to the rise of civilizations such as the Harappan, Mohan-jo-daro, Egyptian, the Mesopotamian, the Aztecs, and Incas.

The first industrial revolution that spanned the period 1760 to 1840 triggered by the invention of the steam engine and the development of railroads, led to development of machines and mechanical production.

The second industrial revolution was triggered by the invention of electricity (in the wake of Thomas Alva Edison's invention of the electric bulb in 1879), followed by the advent of the assembly line. This led to mass production of electric lighting systems, electric generators and turbines.

The third industrial revolution also called the computer or digital revolution started in the 1960s with the advent of electronics and the development of semiconductors, main frame computing and the PC revolution of the 1970s and 1980s, and the advent of the Internet in the 1990s.

Prof Schwab feels that a fourth industrial revolution was ushered in at the turn of the 21st century, building on the digital revolution, with the ushering in of powerful sensors and machine learning, development of gene sequencing, nanotechnologies, and the progress made in the direction of quantum computing. The interaction across physical, biological and societal domains, makes the fourth industrial revolution unique and daunting.

The Second Machine Age

A similar view is taken by Andrew McAfee, Principal Research Scientist, MIT and Erick Brynjolfsson, Professor at MIT Sloan School of Management and Director of the MIT Initiative on Digital Economy, authors of the 'Second Machine Age' (2014) and Machine|Platform|Crowd (2017).

They feel that we are on the threshold of the second machine age (after the industrial revolution) with digital technology reshaping every industry. We are seeing the rise of unicorns and the demise of the Fortune 500 stalwarts. According to them, harnessing the power of the digital future would depend on three factors-- machine, platform and crowd. This is further explained below:

Machine: expanding the capabilities of digital machines powered by Artificial Intelligence such as AlphaGo that defeated the Go champion. Machines have superior data crunching and processing power than the human mind, and have self-learning capabilities, while the human mind excels in judgment and common sense. Mind-machine combination is a necessity of this digital age.

Digital platforms for products (goods and services) as shown by Uber, Airbnb, Alibaba, and Facebook, disrupting industries without having any physical assets.

Harnessing the wisdom and resources of the crowd through crowdfunding and crowd sourcing. GE employed this unconventional development process for its Opal ice maker harnessing online the vast amount of human knowledge, expertise, and financial resources distributed globally. Crowd sourcing would require reengineering and harnessing organizational processes and capabilities within companies and externally with business partners and supply chains.

Crowdfunding

Crowdfunding has led to the growth of many startups. Oculus VR with their gaming headset, was a successful crowdfunded startup. It was acquired by Facebook. Equity crowdfunding became legal with the enactment of the JOBS Act in USA in 2012 intended to promote entrepreneurship and small business growth. It was extended in 2013 to include public equity crowdfunding campaigns.

Some of the successful crowdfunding campaigns include

- Pebble E-Paper Watch, an affordable smart watch) that raised over $10 million in 37 days.
- Ouya, open source game console, raised $ 8.5 million in 29 days via Kickstarter.
- Pono Music, providing a high res music player, raised $ 6 million.
- Bitvore for big data, allows businesses to monitor and analyze large continuous streams of data. They raised $ 4.5 million.
- Dash, the world's first wireless smart in-ear headphones, raised $ 3.4 million in 50 days.
- Formlabs 3D Printer
- Oculus Rift
- 3Doodler, a 3D printing pen
- Canary Smart Home Security that includes an HD video camera and multiple sensors to track motion, temperature, and air quality
- Scanadu Scout, tracks vital physiological signs including temperature, respiratory rate, EKG, and emotional stress, and sends a report via a smartphone. They raised $ 1.66 million in 60 days.

AI and the Rise of the Robots

Humans are moving towards co-existence with intelligent machines leading to a mind-machine partnership. As pointed out by Andrew McAfee and Erick Brynjolfsson in their book Machine|Platform|Crowd (2017):

"Machines aren't simply following carefully coded instructions provided by human programmers; they are learning how to solve problems on their own."

We continue to rely on human judgement when machines can do better data-based analysis. Kahneman in *'Thinking Fast and Slow'* describes how human intuition is prone to errors and cognitive bias. Logical reasoning based on data may be more reliable. It is in logical reasoning and data crunching that machines surpass humans. With a man-machine partnership, decision-making based on data analytics may be very much influenced by machines. Humans have biases, while computers don't. The utility of machines will however depend on the reliability of the algorithms and the validity of the data used for analysis. Ultimately human common sense and judgment must control the decisions arrived at by machines based on algorithmic data analysis. We are increasingly going to rely on artificial intelligence, machine learning, and robotics.

In October 2017, a humanoid robot Sophia was granted citizenship by the government of Saudi Arabia. Sophia, developed by Hong Kong-based Hanson Robotics, was activated in 2015. Since then she graced the stages of 'The Tonight Show with Jimmy Fallon' and the Web Summit in Lisbon, Portugal. She is made of frubber (flesh-like rubber) and is made in the likeness of Audrey Hepburn. Though Sophia gives pre-programmed or semi-programmed answers, she can also give unscripted autonomous answers. Sophia is still under development and has not yet been commercially deployed. Eventually the robot may work as a bank-teller.

THE KNOWLEDGE ECONOMY IN A QUANTUM WORLD

Robots are electro mechanical devices actuated by sensors and computer circuitry controlled by machine learning algorithms. In 1997, IBM DeepBlue defeated Garry Kasparov, the world chess champion. The computer could evaluate 200 million positions per second. In 2011, IBM Watson defeated the Jeopardy champions.

Go, the strategy game, developed in China about 2500 years ago, is considered more difficult than chess. Even Confucius advised that gentlemen should study and play Go. One player uses white stones, the other black. They place the stones on the intersections of a 19x19 grid. Stones surrounded by opposing stones are deemed captured and removed from the board. The player with more captured territory wins. There are about 2 x 10 raised to 170 possible positions on a standard Go board. Go players go by heuristics (rules of thumb) to make their moves. To make that tacit knowledge explicit is difficult.

A team at Google DeepMind, a London-based company specializing in machine learning published in *Nature* magazine the article titled *'Mastering the Game of Go with Deep Neural Networks and Tree Search'*. They built AlphaGo, a Go-playing application, to identify the patterns present in large amounts of data. It used deep learning studying millions of positions to simulate moves leading to victory. In October 2015, AlphaGo defeated Fan Hui the then European Go champion. In March 2016, in a match played in Seoul, South Korea, AlphaGo defeated Lee Sedol, the best human Go player on the planet. This was a turning point in as much as the machine went beyond the point of singularity and surpassing the human mind in data crunching and self-learning.

Artificial intelligence capability has been harnessed in various areas. As Prof Schwab points out, today artificial intelligence is all around us, in the form of autonomous cars, drones, or digital assistants, voice recognition, and translation software, to name a few.

MIT Technology Review July/August 2017 has reported that China is leading the world in the AI race, followed by U.S., England, Australia, Canada, Japan, and Germany. Since 2014 China has published the highest number of research papers on deep learning and other areas of artificial intelligence.

Microsoft, IBM, and Google are the leaders in this area, followed closely by Facebook, Baidu, Amazon, etc.

Platforms

Parker, Van Alstyne, and Choudary (2016) in their book *Platform Revolution'* describe how networked markets driven by the platform revolution, are transforming diverse industries in the digital economy.

Uber, Airbnb, Amazon, PayPal, Apple, and others that have disrupted the markets and become industry leaders, focused on platforms connecting buyers and sellers. The authors call them platform businesses that enable value creation.

The platform provides an open and participative infrastructure for customer interactions facilitating exchange of goods and services.

This contrasts with a pipeline system or a linear value chain from producers to consumers. The web infrastructure platform of the disrupters such as Amazon facilitate interactions and provide more value to the stakeholders.

In the mobile phone industry, Apple's iOS and Google-sponsored Android are the two major platforms.

North America has more platforms creating value. Examples are Google, Apple, Microsoft, Facebook, Amazon, Intel, and Oracle.

Asia has Alibaba, TenCent, Softbank, JD.com, as major ones.

Notable ones in Europe are SAP and Spotify.

In Latin America and Africa, NASPERS is notable.

Some of the industry sectors and companies being transformed by platform businesses are listed by them:

Industry	Examples
Agriculture	John Deere, Intuit, FASAL
Communication and Networking	LinkedIn, Facebook, Twitter, Tinder, Instagram, Snapchat, WeChat
Consumer Goods	Philips, McCormick Foods
Education	Udemy, Skillshare, Coursera, edX, Duolingo,

	Khan Academy
Heavy Industry	Nest, Tesla, Powerwall, General Electric, EnerNOC
Finance	Bitcoin, Lending Club, Kickstarter
Healthcare	Cohealo, SimplyInsured, Kaiser Permanente
Gaming	Xbox, Nintendo, PlayStation
Labor and Professional Services	Upwork, Fiverr, LegalZoom
Local Services	Yelp, Foursquare, Groupon, Angie's List
Logistics and Delivery	Munchery, Foodpanda, Haier Group
Media	Medium, Viki, YouTube, Wikipedia, Huffington Post, Kindle Publishing
Operating Systems	iOS, Android, MacOS, Microsoft Windows. LINUX
Retail	Amazon, Alibaba, Walgreens, Burberry,

	Shopkick
Transportation	Uber, Waze, Lyft, GrabTaxi, Ola Cabs
Travel	Airbnb, TripAdvisor

These new platforms disrupt traditional business management practices including strategy, operations, marketing, production, research and development, and human resources.

Technological innovation drives the platform business. Application Programming Interfaces (APIs) facilitate access by external entities to core resources. Examples: Google Maps, Salesforce, Twitter, Thomson Reuters Eikon, Amazon Marketplace, Amazon SimpleDB, Amazon S3, Amazon RDS, Amazon SC2, Amazon DynamoDB, Amazon Cloudwatch, Amazon Mechanical Turk, Amazon Redshift, Amazon SNS, Alexa Web Inform. Amazon provides several APIs to its core resources in comparison to its competitor Walmart.

The power of the platform is described by them as 'network effects' referring to the impact that platform users have on the value created for each user. This further leads to competitive advantage.

Augmenting Platform business value

Innovation and data analytics extend the network effects, value creation, and competitive advantage of platform businesses. Mergers and acquisitions help in adding complementary products or market access and in reducing supply chain costs.

Exponential Organizations

Salim Ismail, founding Executive Director of Singularity University, along with Michael S. Malone and Yuri Van Geest, in their book *'Exponential Organizations'* (2014) point out how the giant corporations are today competing with new startups that use 'exponential technologies' or technologies that create exponential change, to accelerate their growth. According to them these new organizations are ten times better, faster, and cheaper than the rest. They leverage social media, big data and data analytics, machine learning algorithms, and new technologies like Internet of Things, cloud computing, biotech, or robotics. These exponential organizations are trying to solve the world's biggest challenging problems, to change the world, using innovative technologies. Big Companies are trying to be forward-thinking and adapting to the rapid technological changes by building ExOs (Exponential Organizations). They start with a new vision and purpose (similar to startups), what the authors call as 'Massive Transformative Purpose' (MTP). An example given is Coco-Cola Company with an MTP to 'refresh the world', adopting an innovative business model.

Uberization & Spotification

Uber and Spotify are typical examples of the emergence of not only disruptive technologies but disruptive organizational life styles that call for a relook at management and leadership in the digital age.

Uber was founded in March 2009 by Travis Kalanick and

THE KNOWLEDGE ECONOMY IN A QUANTUM WORLD

Garrett Camp in San Francisco, California. They developed a software-- the Uber app-- that could disrupt the transport business of the taxi transport sector, to provide faster, cheaper and more efficient service to the consumer.

With the Uber app installed on their smartphones, the consumers can request a trip. The software sends the request to the nearest Uber driver, directing the driver to the location of the consumer identified by the satellite GPS (Global Positioning System). The application calculates the fare and transfers payment to the driver on completion of the journey. The consumer can see on the smartphone screen the driver's name, vehicle number, how far away the vehicle is, and can see the map and vehicle's path to reach the customer's target location. The Uber app was officially launched in 2011.

In 2014, in an agreement with the Chinese search engine Baidu, the Uber app was linked to Baidu's search engine map and mobile search features. Google Ventures also invested in Uber in 2013. Toyota also invested in Uber to help the Uber drivers in exploring leasing options.

Uber's revenue in 2015 was 1.5 billion, without owning a single car. All the Uber drivers are independent business partners or contractors and not employees of Uber.

Uber has funded Carnegie Mellon's research into self-driven cars. The company is also exploring helicopter service in collaboration with Airbus.

Spotify

Spotify with its tagline 'music for everyone' is a Swedish company that was founded by Daniel Ek and Martin Lorentzon in 2006, but officially launched in 2008. It is disrupting the music industry, focusing on music, video, and podcast streaming. It has 140 million users with 70 million paying customers. It provides access to more than 30 million songs. Spotify has a unique corporate environment and autonomous organizational structure to promote innovation, and alignment to corporate goals without excessive control. It now has offices in 20 countries around the world and has also tied up with Tencent Holdings in China. There are Spotify communities for Artists and for specific music brands. Spotify also promotes specific communities for web developers of music streaming for various mobile and computing platforms.

Spotify's approximately 2000 employees are organized into agile teams called squads. These squads are self-organizing, cross-functional, and co-located. Each squad is responsible for a specific area of the product, owning it from cradle to grave. Squads have authority to decide what to build, how to build it, and with whom to work with. They call their organizational set up as a light matrix, referred to by them as 'tribe'.

Each organizational tribe has several squads linked together through a chapter or a horizontal grouping, that helps to support specific competencies such as quality assurance, agile coaching, web development, to name a few. The chapter facilitates learning and competency development. The chapter leader is a formal manager focusing on coaching and mentoring. Members can switch between squads, while retaining their chapter leader.

A third organizational element acting as the higher-level leadership is the guild or lightweight communities of interest helping to share and advance knowledge. Guilds have autonomy and accountability.

Netflix

While Spotify focuses on music and songs, Netflix is an entertainment company, focusing on movies. It was founded in 1997 in Scotts Valley, California by Reed Hastings (with a Master's degree in computer science from Stanford University) and Marc Randolph. It provides streaming media and video on demand online and on DVD by mail. It has expanded into film and TV production and film distribution. Netflix has today 93 million subscribers in 190 countries. Every minute, Netflix customers stream 69,444 hours of video.

Its original business model was based on DVD rentals by mail, capitalizing on the fast spread of DVD players in US households. The bricks-and-mortar retailers (like Blockbuster) could not compete with their 50 cents rental model or later the flat fee model for unlimited rentals. Later Netflix introduced the video on demand via the Internet. It has continued as a successful dot-com venture. Netflix was able to disrupt the business model of Blockbuster (with revenue of $3 Billion). It relies heavily on data analytics to analyze customer behavior and buying patterns. Netflix ensures a personalized web page for every customer.

AirbNb

Headquartered in San Francisco, California, Airbnb was founded in October 2007 by Brian Chesky, Joe Gebbia, and Nathan Blecharczyk. It is an online travel platform, 'the home-sharing platform', for accommodations around the world. It has over 2 million listings in 34,000 cities in 191 countries. Gallagher, Leigh tells their story in his book *"The Airbnb Story- How three ordinary guys disrupted an industry, made billions... and created plenty of controversy." (2017).*

It has been a disrupter of the travel and accommodation industry. It is a peer-to-peer online marketplace for listing and renting short-term lodging with the cost determined by the property owner. The company receives service fees from both the guests and the hosts. It connects hosts and travelers through its website airbnb.com.

After teething troubles during 2007-2008, it had to go through the 'product/market fit test' to get Angel investors. With the initial funding, the company had to organize itself with a business plan, roadmap, strategy and the initial crew of staff.

Its product was the website, listing the homes for hire.

Steve Job's three click rule had to be applied to make the website useful for the customers -- both the renters and the guests.

It evolved from a WordPress website into what it is today catering to hundreds of millions of customers. The site also had to cater to customer service, payments, and reviews. The website also had to provide search capabilities.

The initial user experience initially was terrible. They started using Amazon Web Services for hosting and payment services. Later it relied on PayPal for an end-to-end payment system.

Safety became an important consideration for home-sharing after some reported safety incidents.

Elon Musk, the architect of tomorrow

Ashlee Vance writing about Elon Musk, in his book '*Elon Musk*' (2015) says, "Turning humans into space colonizers is his stated life's purpose". Born in South Africa, Musk is today considered almost a deity in Silicon Valley, adored by many and despised by many, but is considered 'bold, inspiring, and a little crazy'. He is apparently one of the most innovative industrialists in America, after Thomas Edison and Howard Hughes.

Elon Musk dropped out of the Ph.D. program at Stanford University in 1995 and started his first Internet venture Zip2, an online city guide. For this startup venture, he raised funding from a group of angel investors of Silicon Valley. He sold it in 1998 and from the sale proceeds of $22 million, he partnered with Peter Thiel in March 1999, he co-founded X.com (which later became PayPal), an online bank and money-transfer service.

When PayPal was acquired by eBay in October 2002, he received $180 million. With this money he started SpaceX (for $100 million), Tesla for $70 million, and Solar City with $10 million. He is currently CEO of *Tesla*, *SpaceX*, *Hyperloop*, and *Solar City*—all billion-dollar companies.

60

Neuralink and *OpenAI*, founded by him, are two other companies that are not so well known. OpenAI is a nonprofit focused on minimizing the dangers of artificial intelligence. Neuralink focuses on implantable technologies for creating mind-computer interfaces.

He calls himself an engineer and technologist. He is considered one of the most innovative business persons in the world and is called 'the architect of tomorrow'. He plans to inhabit outer space, revolutionize high-speed transportation with his Hyperloop, and reinvent cars using his electric car Tesla. To relieve traffic congestion in cities, through his *Boring Company* his approach is to build a honeycomb of underground tunnels with electric skates for cars and commuters. He intends to create the mind-computer interface to enhance human health and brainpower.

But he is an opponent of the rise of AI. He warns against the future threat of AI that may try to eliminate the irrational human species. He is focused on humankind's quest to conquer distance and time. Admittedly, he was influenced from his boyhood by Isaac Asimov, popular scientist and science fiction writer. His vision is to change the world and humanity. His goals include reducing global warming through development of sustainable energy. Just like Steve Jobs, as a workaholic, he has a 'maniacal attention to detail', and a demanding management style and work ethic with ninety-plus-hour workweeks.

Musk aspires to conquer the solar system through his SpaceX, using reusable rockets. He plans colonization of Mars in the foreseeable future. SpaceX's unmanned missions to Mars are scheduled to start in 2018, a robotic mission in 2020, and the human mission is scheduled for 2024.

The Big Five & the Challengers

According to MIT Technology Review (July / August 2017), the Big Five of the digital economy – Apple, Alphabet, Microsoft, Amazon, and Facebook—have been the most valuable companies of the world during the last decade (2007-2017). These companies dominate the digital economy since they have massive user base and customer base globally. Third party sellers are gravitating to Amazon. Advertisers flock to Google (Alphabet). Facebook's global network of daily users exceeds 1.5 billion, making it an advertiser's haven. The iPhones, iPad, and the MAC still rule the market.

The market capitalization of these companies is also enormous. Apple has $ 807 billion, Alphabet (Google) $ 690 Billion, Microsoft $ 559 Billion, Amazon $ 484 Billion, and Facebook $ 447 Billion of capital assets as in 2017. They also have huge cash reserves, enabling them to acquire start-up companies rapidly.

Facebook

With the vision for "connecting the world", Facebook today rules the world of social networking. Facebook, Facebook Messenger, and Instagram are part of the Facebook group. Facebook acquired WhatsApp (a five-year old, fifty-employee, instant messaging company) for $20 billion in 2016.

Facebook is a huge marketing and advertising platform. Each of the 1.86 billion users has a personalized web page with personal content. Each page can be targeted by advertisers.

Facebook is today a part of the daily lives of nearly 1.5 billion people around the world, through its personalized newsfeed. In the book *'Becoming Facebook—The 10 Challenges That Defined the Company That is Disrupting the World'*, Mike Hoefflinger tells the insider's story of how Facebook and the Mark Zuckerberg team propelled Facebook into a global leader since its inception in 2004, facing many challenges including Yahoo's takeover bid for $ 1 billion in 2006, and a flopped IPO in 2012. Along the way, Facebook introduced advertising into its news feed. Smartphones propelled Facebook into an era of growth through infrastructure building involving hardware, software, networks, buildings, and energy. Facebook's guiding principle is 'disrupt yourself before someone else does'. As Hoefflinger points out Facebook is a global connector and influences people in Africa, Southeast Asia, Columbia, Egypt, and India, more than it does to people in the United States.

By 2018, Facebook will have seven data centers around the world in Oregon, North Carolina, Iowa, Texas, New Mexico in US, in Sweden and Ireland. Facebook's mobile internet traffic bandwidth needs are growing at a rapid pace, competing with its nearest rival Google. Facebook is today one of the premier cloud operators in the world, along with IBM, Google, Apple, Microsoft, and Amazon.

In 2016, Facebook launched the AMOS-9 satellite to

expand internet connectivity in Sub-Saharan Africa. Facebook is experimenting with various technologies such as drones and unmanned aerial vehicles (UAV), to connect the next five billion people on this planet to the internet. In this effort Facebook has tied up with AT&T, Verizon, Deutsche Telekom, and SK Telecom.

In the book *'The Four- The Hidden DNA of Amazon, Apple, Facebook, and Google"* (2017), Scott Gallaway analyzes the rise and significance of the four technology giants that are remaking the world, while behemoths such as IBM and HP are aging. They point to the alarming concern that these four behemoths control information and knowledge in the world, including privacy information.

Amazon

Amazon, the online retailer, is the earth's biggest store, providing almost everything to the consumer at the point of a click. Today 52% of US households are Amazon Prime members. Brad Stone's *'Everything Store'* (2013) tells the story of Jeff Bezos and his creation of Amazon in 1995 as an online book seller.

Jeff Bezos capitalized on the technological shift in retail business and the consumer society in 1994 jumping onto the e-commerce bandwagon. Since then he has diversified from books and DVDs to almost everything that the consumer needs, all serviced by amazon.com web portal. The company was able to survive the dot-com bust of 2000.

Jeff Bezos has implemented robotics in his warehouses and fulfillment centers. Amazon Go implemented in 2016 is a brick-and-mortar business providing 'no cashier' stores. Sensors scan your bags, and the payment application automatically makes the payment, as you walk out. There is no check-out. Is this application going to put 3.4 million cashiers in USA out of job?

Amazon Echo with its Artificial Intelligence engine Alexa (named after the Library of Alexandria) acts as a digital assistant and personal communicator. The Echo is powered by powerful speech recognition software. Amazon is also leveraging Big Data for analyzing consumer preferences and consumer purchasing patterns. Amazon is poised to rule the retail world with heaps of data about consumers and consumer behavior.

One of the core competencies of Amazon is robotics. In 2012, Amazon acquired Kiva Systems, a warehouse robotics firm for $ 775 million. In June 2017, Amazon acquired Whole Foods, and has indicated its intention to get into transport sector (leasing Boeing 757s, deploying drones, and getting into shipping).

Amazon Web Services provides cloud computing infrastructure and big data analytics.

Sephora, Best Buy, and Home Depot are fighting the Amazon onslaught on retail business, by investing in people and their expertise, presenting human capital as a value-add vis-a-vis mindless technology.

Apple

Apple is best known for the Macintosh PC, the iPod, and the IPhone. Apple has been on the forefront of the smartphone revolution.

The Apple iPhone released in the US on June 29, 2007 initiated a wave of innovation in mobile computing. Apple entered the scene that was dominated by mobile giants such as Nokia, Motorola, and the BlackBerry. It had full-touch interactive display. Apple revolutionized the User Interface and user interaction doing away with use of physical keys. The Appstore was another innovation. More than just calls and text, people started using mobile apps. Apple redefined the mobile phone ushering in the era of smart phones with touchscreen phones and app stores. HTC, Samsung, Motorola, LG, Sony-Ericsson, and others followed suit. Today Apple Appstore has over 2.2 million apps. Google Play Store reportedly has more than 2.7 million apps.

Apple released its iPhone 8 and iPhone X in October 2017.

With cameras, GPS, and apps such as WhatsApp, Snapchat, and Uber, the smartphone has become an essential part of the lives of the common man everywhere around the world.

Apple focuses on high-end laptops and mobile devices, mostly catering to the luxury market.

The company controls 14.5 per cent of the global smartphone market. The Apple Macintosh computer launched in 1984 defined technological luxury. The iPhone and iPad are sought after by those who value a trusted luxury brand. In 2015, Apple launched the Apple Watch. Steve Jobs, the founder, has been an icon of innovation. The iPhone launched in 2007 dealt a lethal blow to Nokia and Motorola. Apple is still considered the most innovative company in the world.

Google

Google is focused on "organizing the world's information'. It acts as a source of knowledge and is de-facto the god of information in the digital age. In 1998, two Stanford graduate students Sergey Brin and Larry Page designed a web tool, a 'search engine', to crawl the internet using keywords to answer search queries on any topic.

Eric Schmidt, after a stint with Sun Microsystems and Novell, became CEO of Google and turned it into a power horse to organize the world's information.

Google Maps, Google Sky, Google Earth, Google Oceans, Google Library Project, and Google News expanded the world of online knowledge. Google's entry into the smartphone world with the Google Android platform, posed a challenge to Apple's iPhone. The Google Chrome posed the greatest challenge to Microsoft's browser the Microsoft Explorer and the Edge.

Microsoft

Microsoft dominated the PC era. Windows still powers 90 percent of installed desktop computers. Microsoft Office is still the dominant productivity suite. SQL Server and Visual Studio are still prominent.

Microsoft acquired LinkedIn, the professional networking site. Azure, the Microsoft Cloud is still sought after. Microsoft now focuses on the enterprise as against the consumer.

THE KNOWLEDGE ECONOMY IN A QUANTUM WORLD

Microsoft is a dominant player today in cloud computing with its Microsoft Azure Cloud. As pointed out by Satya Nadella, CEO of Microsoft, Microsoft's three thrust areas in addition to its existing portfolio today are Artificial Intelligence, Mixed Reality, and Quantum Computing.

The Challengers

Others like **Netflix** and **Alibaba** are close on the heels of the big five technology giants for domination of the digital technology market. Some of the other dominant challengers are:

1) **IBM**: The Big Blue was the de facto standard for Corporate America and dominated the first quarter century of personal computers, along with Intel and Microsoft. Its dominance is shifting to cloud computing, quantum computing, and AI services, particularly in healthcare and financial services with its IBM Watson technology.

2) **Alibaba:** In April 2016, Jack Ma's Alibaba, the Chinese online commerce company became the world's largest retailer (beating Walmart) with $485 billion in gross revenue. It is a market place for other retailers-- e-commerce and shopping, online auctions, money transfers, and cloud data services. Alibaba collects a fraction of that revenue ($15 billion in 2016).

3) **Tesla:** Tesla is going full steam into manufacture of lithium ion batteries, electric cars, autonomous cars, space technology and reusable rockets, and into brain computing.

4) Uber has revolutionized the transport industry.

5) Walmart with 12,000 stores in 28 countries is using big data analytics and is poised to use robotics for logistics and supply chain.

6) Airbnb, the Uber for hotels is using big data analytics to disrupt the travel and accommodation industries.

7) Verizon/AT&T/Comcast/Time Warner
These cable and telco companies are essential players in the digital age.

Since the focus here has been on the digital business scenario, technology challengers or technology creators such as IBM, Intel, Qualcomm, etc. have not been discussed here.

China, the digital frontier of the world

McKinsey Global Institute (MGI), in their paper *'China's Digital Economy- A Leading Global Force'* (August 2017), points out that the Chinese economy today is more digital than the rest of the world, and China may be the world's next digital frontier. The three internet companies Baidu, Alibaba, and Tencent (referred to as BAT) are creating a multi-industry digital ecosystem. The Chinese government actively supports digital innovation and entrepreneurship.

China is a global leader in e-commerce and digital payments and is home to one-third of the world's unicorns. The word 'unicorn' refers to a start-up company valued at more than a billion dollars. Investments by unicorns, typically in key digital technology areas, as reported by MGI in 2016, are indicated below, for leading countries. The figures indicate investments in millions of US Dollars.

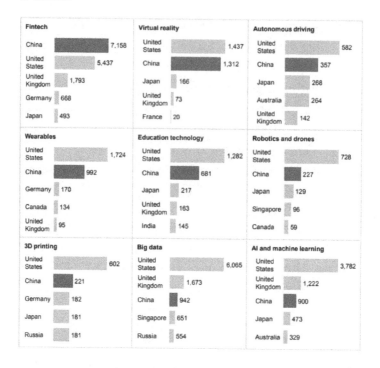

Fig: Courtesy: McKinsey Global Institute

The massive scale of markets, and the opportunities to offer digital technologies in the place of existing inefficient systems, are major drivers for the digital revolution in China. How the major Chinese player Alibaba's payment system compares with that of the US competitor, and how the computing power of BAT compares with that of Yahoo are indicated by McKinsey Global Institute (MGI) in the diagrams shown below:

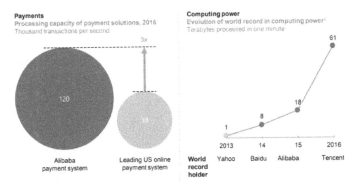

i According to an assessment of how much data can be processed in a minute in terms of general sorting.

SOURCE: Company official announcements; Profit Confidential; 360doc; Alizala; Sankei; Sort Benchmark; McKinsey Global Institute analysis

Fig: Courtesy: McKinsey Global Institute

Voice recognition systems and solutions to enable secure payment, access control, and hands-free operations, are gaining popularity in China because of the difficulties in typing in Chinese language on mobile phones.

China is expanding globally through mergers and acquisitions, global partnerships, and through export of its digital technologies and services.

The Chinese BAT

Baidoo, Alibaba, and Tencent, collectively called BAT, have radically transformed the digital scenario in China.

Baidu

Baidu, founded in 2000 by Robin Li and Eric Xu, is a Chinese web services company, and is the eighth largest internet company by revenue. It is also one of the premier AI leaders in the world. It has the second largest search engine in the world, next to Google. *Baidu Brain*, is an artificial neural network-based voice recognition system

71

with 97% accuracy, and facial recognition system with 99.7% accuracy rate. *Baidu Cloud* is a cloud computing service providing AI and Big Data services. *Baidu Baike* is an online encyclopedia similar to Wikipedia. The company also hosts a music service *Baidu Music*. Baidu also has an autonomous driving (self-driving) program. *Baidu Waimai* is a food delivery service. Its *DuerOS* is a widely used conversational AI platform in the world.

Alibaba, Chinese e-commerce conglomerate, was founded in 1999 by Jack Ma to connect Chinese manufacturers with overseas buyers. The $25 billion initial public offering of shares in Alibaba group in September 2014 was the largest IPO in history.

After 18 years (in 2017), it is the world's largest retailer, surpassing Walmart, with operations in 200 countries. It crossed the US$400 billion value mark in 2017. Jack Ma calls Alibaba an ecosystem that empowers small businesses, using internet technologies and web portals. He calls Alibaba a data company that uses big data for fighting piracy and fake products, promoting credit rating and advancing loans to small businesses. The Sesame credit rating system was developed by Alibaba for renting cars, renting houses, or for getting loans from financial institutions. Alibaba is now focusing on the 2H strategy focusing on Health and Happiness for all. Alibaba's business strategy is in stark contrast to Amazon's, since Amazon is heavy on physical assets.

TenCent Holdings

TenCent Holdings, China, developed the WeChat messaging app. Founded in 1998 by Ma Huateng, Zhang

Zhidong, Xu Chenye, Chen Yidan, and Zeng Liqing, it is registered in Cayman Islands, but headquartered in Shezhen, China. Its products suite includes social networking, instant messaging, mass media, web portals (qq.com), e-commerce, antivirus software, AI, music, payment system, film production, and online games. Its music service has more than 700 million users. It is also an investment corporation with focus on tech start-ups in Asia.

JD.Com

JD.com also known as Jingdong (formerly 360buy) is a Chinese e-commerce company headquartered in Beijing. It competes with Alibaba's Tmall. It was founded in 1998 and the B2C platform is active since 2004. It uses delivery using drones, autonomous technology, and robots. Its drone delivery system and infrastructure are one of the largest in the world. It is venturing into robotic delivery and autonomous vehicle delivery.

India's Digital Economy

India's digital economy is still in a nascent stage and yet to take off in a significant manner. Harvard Business Review in its Digital Evolution Index 2017, surveying the digital state of 60 countries, indicates that the Indian digital economy is being driven by 462 million Internet users, compared to China's 721 million Internet user base. With a population of 1.29 billion, India is in the break out zone of global digital economy.

Fig: Courtesy: HBR

Flipkart is India's largest online retailer. Amazon.in is also penetrating the online retail market. Bengaluru is the emerging center for e-commerce and digital technologies in India. Delhi/NCR, Mumbai, Pune, Hyderabad, and Chennai are close on heel.

In Q3 2017, four companies Pi Datacenters, Flipkart, Just Buy Live, and Druva secured $3 Billion in funding for digital start-up ventures.

BYJU'S, Flipkart, Ezetap, CapitalFloat, Treebo Hotel, Medgeome, and 111 startups funded by the Karnataka government are trendsetters of India's digital economy.

A major step in India's march towards the digital economy was the launch in 2009 of Aadhaar (a national unique digital identity system). It is intended to provide a single digital identity in the form of a biometric-authenticated 12-

digit number (similar to the social security number in USA).

As a result, digital payments and fintech are catching up in India. India is still a cash-dominated society. A digital campaign was launched in July 2015. The Aadhar number of an individual is now required to be linked with the bank accounts and the mobile phone of the individual. This will help to make digital banking in India a reality, because the bank accounts and payment systems in India are still paper-based requiring laborious Know Your Customer validation procedures.

In the digital payments arena, platforms such as UPI (Universal Payment Interface) and products such as BHIM app are helping to fuel the digital revolution in India.

A downside is that increasing incidents of cybercrimes are posing a threat to adoption of digital payments. The data breach involving around 120 million users of the Internet data provider Reliance Jio is a case in point. Further, India is yet to develop a reliable and fast digital infrastructure. Major areas of focus must be technology adoption in government, education, healthcare, banking, manufacturing, and critical infrastructure sectors for India to usher in a digital economy.

Disruptive Technologies

Disruption means a rapid change to the status quo. Today we are seeing transformational changes to our individual lives, societies, organizations, businesses, and nations globally. These changes are spurred by innovative technologies. Understanding these technologies and managing them would be a tough challenge. It would hold the key to corporate and human survival in the emerging quantum age.

We are already moving into the smart technology era with smart cities, connected smart devices, Internet of Things or Internet of Everything. New Internet technologies promote cloud-based services or computing as a utility or service. Networks of sensors monitoring wearables (iGlass, iWatch, smart apparel, and smart shoes) or heart implants help to monitor and improve human health. We are rapidly moving into a world of sensors, sensing and monitoring every aspect of our lives through devices or machines we interact with. Even our identification is being linked to RFID (Radio Frequency Identification) chips which can be implanted on smart cards or even under a person's skin.

Quantum computing and cognitive computing are taking computing power to higher levels of performance. Robots are fast replacing manual and routine labor in factories. Similar disruptive technologies are emerging fast.

How do we manage these emergent technologies and leverage the emerging business opportunities provided by smart technologies?

Klaus Schwab in his book '*The Fourth Industrial Revolution*' has referred extensively to the World Economic Forum's survey '*Deep Shift – Technology Tipping Points and Social Impact*' published in September 2015. The survey lists 23 technology shifts. They are summarized below:

1. **Implantable technologies** such as pacemakers and cochlear implants, and other healthcare devices implanted into human bodies, would enable communications, location and behavior monitoring, and health functions. Smart tattoos and chips could help with identification and location. An implanted smart phone could communicate thoughts and moods. A smart pill developed by Proteus Biomedical and Novartis has a biodegradable digital device transmitting details of the impact of the medication. An implantable mobile phone is expected to be available by 2025. (Ref: wtvox.com, cen.acs.org)

2. **Digital Presence and Social Interactions**: By 2025, 80% of the people in the world are expected to have a digital presence on the Internet. Beyond having a mobile phone number, email id or website, people are now interacting digitally through social media such as Facebook, Twitter, blogs, Instagram, etc. People share information, ideas, and connect with people anywhere around the world, building relationships and leaving social footprints in several places. This can help in targeted information and news, and targeted advertising. But it may also impact privacy and lead to more identity theft.

3. **Visual Interfaces & Augmented Reality**: Smart glasses such as Google Glass can augment the visual sensation, enabling augmented reality, and help to connect to the internet and other connected devices, through the visual interfaces.

4. **Wearable Internet:** Apple and Google released

their smart watches in 2015. The smart watch is connected to the Internet and has many functionalities similar to a smartphone. Internet-enabled clothes with embedded chips in clothing will connect the person wearing it to the Internet. Mimo Baby is a wearable baby monitor. (www.mimobaby.com). A sports shirt can monitor real-time workout data. (www.ralphlauren.com).

5. **Ubiquitous Computing**: Advances in wireless communications will make Internet access available to anyone around the world. Internet access will become a basic human right. This will enable easy access to education, healthcare, and government services online, and expand e-commerce markets. Facebook's internet.org initiative is intended to provide free basic internet services to several under-developed regions in Africa, Asia, and South-America, using Internet drones. Google's Project Loon uses balloons and SpaceX is focusing on low-cost satellite networks.

6. **Smart Phones, the Pocket Supercomputers**: In 1985, the Cray-2 supercomputer was the fastest machine in the world. The iPhone4, released in 2010, had computing power equal to that of a Cray-2 machine. The Apple Watch has the equivalent speed of two iPhone 4s. A Google study (www.google.com.sg/publicdata/explore) revealed that countries such as UAE, Singapore, Korea, Saudi Arabia, Taiwan, Spain, China, and Hong Kong have higher smartphone usage than PCs. Technology is now shifting to miniature devices such as smart phones and tablets, with

increasing computing power, and decreasing price of electronics. Countries such as Singapore, South Korea, and the UAE have almost 90% of the adult population using smartphones.

7. **Cloud Storage:** Cost of hard drives and storage devices has decreased tremendously. This has led to free cloud storage being offered by companies such as Google, Amazon, Dropbox, etc. This leads to an explosion of data content in the cloud. Such data can be used for analysis for commercial purposes.

8. **Internet of Things**: Intelligent sensor technology will enable connected devices to communicate. In the future every physical object could be connected using sensors to ubiquitous communication infrastructure for enabling monitoring. More than 50 billion devices are expected to be connected to the internet by 2020.

9. **Connected Home:** Home automation is shifting to connecting devices to controlling lighting, ventilation, air conditioning, audio and video, security systems, kitchen and other home appliances such as refrigerators, washers, dryers, with sensors and robots for vacuum cleaning or even cooking. Better resource efficiency with lower energy use and costs, remote home control, are some of the intended benefits.

10. **Smart Cities :** Think of a city with no traffic lights to control traffic. Cities such as Singapore and Barcelona are implementing data-driven services such as intelligent parking, trash collection, lighting etc. They use sensor technology and data analytics

systems for predictive modeling.

11. **Big Data for Decisions:** Big Data analytics is helping businesses and organizations to make data-driven decision making.

12. **Driverless Cars:** Autonomous cars are considered safer and will be hitting the roads in 2018.

13. **Artificial Intelligence and Decision Making:** Machine learning algorithms as applied to big data analytics will help managers make better decisions. The first AI machine on a corporate board of directors is expected by 2025. AI machines are rational, have less bias, and can make data-driven decisions. Computer CPUs are expected to have the same level of processing power as the human brain by 2025. Deep Knowledge Ventures, a Hong Kong-based venture capital fund, has recommended VITAL (Validating Investment Tool for Advancing Life Sciences), an investment tool based on AI to its board of directors.

14. **AI and White-Collar Jobs:** AI will replace many job functions performed today by people. Frey & Osborne, in their study, 'The Future of Employment: How Susceptible are Jobs to Computerization?' (Sept 17, 2013) indicates that 47% of the US jobs existing as in 2010, particularly white-collar jobs, are likely to be replaced by intelligent machines in the next 10 to 20 years. It may lead to cost-reduction and increased efficiencies. But the job losses, accountability, and liabilities, are negative impacts.

15. **Robotics and Services:** Intelligent machines are being deployed in the services sector. We can

expect to see robotic lawyers, physicians, nurses, and even teachers in the near future. The first robotic pharmacist is expected by 2025.

16. **Bitcoin and the BlockChain:** The block chain technology and crypto currencies will revolutionize the financial services sector in the coming decades. New services and value exchanges for tradable assets may be created using block chain technology without the need for intermediaries.

17. **The Sharing Economy:** Zipcar, Turo, Uber, Lyft, have transformed the transport sector by promoting shared use of transport services, shifting the focus from ownership to sharing of physical goods or assets. Airbnb also works on the same business model. Uber is today the largest provider of transportation without owning a single car.

18. **Governments and the BlockChain:** Blockchain technology will be increasingly used by governments for identity management, motor vehicle registration and IDs, voter registration and electronic voting, registration of title deeds to property, incorporation of business, and will usher in the era of 'smart contracts'.

19. **3D Printing and Manufacturing:** 3D Printing will revolutionize manufacturing.

20. **3D Printing and Human Health:** 3D printing will be used to create replaceable human parts such as ears, teeth, bones, joins, and even the heart and liver. Titanium powder could be used for making bones. This could address the problem of shortage of donated organs.

21. **3D Printing and Consumer Products:** 3D printing will be used for manufacturing on demand, locally, many of the consumer products such as toys, customized wear, textiles, jewelry, etc. A 3D Printer could become a home or office appliance.

22. **Designer Beings:** Advances in genomics and gene editing techniques could lead to creation of designer beings—humans whose genome is directly edited before birth.

23. **Neuro-technologies:** Advances in neuro technologies could lead to developments in brain computing or computing by thought. Humans could have a fully artificial memory implanted in their brain. The major initiatives in this direction are:

- European Commission's Human Brain Project.
- Brain Research through Advancing Innovative Neuro-technologies (BRAIN) in USA, started by President Obama.

Next generation computers will have the capability to reason, predict, and react like the neurons in the human cortex of the human brain. DARPA has a program Restoring Active Memory (RAM) for memory restoration and enhancement.

The Evolution of Enterprise Technology

The major technologies that will impact our lives in the next ten years are artificial intelligence and robotics,

Internet of Everything (IoE), Big Data and Cloud Computing.

MuleSoft, a software company based in San Francisco, CA, USA, published their *'Connectivity Benchmark Report -Digital Transformation in Today's Enterprise'* in January 2017, based on a November 2016 survey of 951 IT decision makers in USA, UK, Germany, France, Netherlands, Sweden, Australia, Singapore, and China. MuleSoft is focused on application networks and an API-led approach to Enterprise connectivity using their *Anypoint Platform* for customers, employees, and business partners.

Their survey indicates that cloud and mobile computing are seen as key to the future of business. The technologies that may impact business are:

- Cloud Computing
- Mobile Computing
- Remote Sensors (IoT)
- AI/machine learning
- 3D Printing
- Advanced Robotics
- Nanotechnology
- Blockchain
- Drones
- Chatbots (Chatbot is a computer program enabling communication in natural language. The software reads and writes text, can understand verbal commands, and can also speak). It essentially is a speech recognition software. Chatbots act as voice-activated interface for smartphones. Websites use

them for customer assistance. Chatbots are incorporated into personal assistants such as Siri or Alexa.

The major challenges identified are Business – IT alignment and security.

Satya Nadella, CEO of Microsoft in his book *'Hit Refresh'* (2017) looks at technologies beyond the cloud and mentions three shifts or the three key industries that will shape economy and society in the future. They are mixed reality, artificial intelligence, and quantum computing.

In mixed reality the digital world and physical world converge. Artificial intelligence will augment human power with insights and predictive power beyond human capabilities. Quantum computing is the next wave of computing that will change 'the physics of computing' to solve complex problems that cannot be solved by today's computing processing power.

The Key Enablers

It may be worthwhile to mention here the key drivers and enablers of the knowledge-based economy:

- Knowledge or Intellectual Capital
- Creativity & Innovation
- Systems Thinking

Any digital transformation must consider these factors. People and their knowledge, expertise, skills and experience constitute the biggest asset for any enterprise.

Only if creativity and innovation are promoted and a conducive environment is created within organizations, continuous improvement and innovation will take place. Otherwise organizations will be swept off the ground and will become corporate dinosaurs.

Promoting a systems view will help to analyze issues within a broader context of systems, subsystems, and super-systems, to find solutions to complex problems.

PART II
CORE TECHNOLOGIES

"Any sufficiently advanced technology is indistinguishable from magic" Arthur C. Clarke, Science Fiction Writer and Futurist

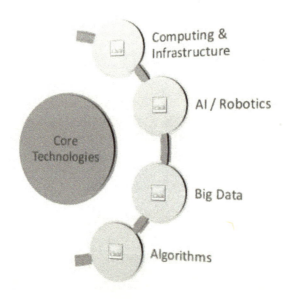

Chapter 3

WHITHER COMPUTING?

What are the core technologies that are creating disruptive changes in the digital landscape?

Quantum computing, Cloud computing, Mobile Communication technologies, Internet of Things (Internet of Everything), robotics, artificial intelligence, big data analytics, and machine learning algorithms are ushering in a new era in computing, leading to 'the fourth industrial revolution', 'the second machine age', and the quantum age.

Super Computing

Supercomputers using massively parallel architecture are used today for highly computing intensive applications such as molecular modeling, weather forecasting, scientific and astronomical research, oil and gas exploration, etc. The IBM Blue Gene/P or "Intrepid" supercomputer at Argonne National Laboratory runs 164,000 massively parallel processors. It has been used to simulate 1.6 billion neurons of the human cerebral cortex, with approximately 9 trillion connections.

The supercomputing race has been on since the 1960s As detailed in IEEE Spectrum, January 2018, USA was the supercomputing leader in 2012, with its Cray Titan at the Oak Ridge Laboratory, Tennessee, that had a processing power at 27 petaflops (i.e 27 x 10^{15}) per second. In 2012 itself China released Tianhhe-2 (Milky Way 2) that was faster than Titan. In 2015 China's Sunway TaihuLight became the world's most powerful supercomputer with peak performance of 125 petaflops. China was able to use this supercomputer for atmospheric modeling. US is now planning to unfurl Summit that will replace Titan. Summit will have 200 petaflops at performance. Many other supercomputers are planned for release by Lawrence Livermore National Laboratory, California, and the Argonne National Laboratory.

In Europe, the fastest computer (Wired, November 2017) is the MareNostrum using the latest Intel processors. It is housed in a deconsecrated chapel on the outskirts of Barcelona, Spain. Built by Lenovo and managed by Barcelona Supercomputing Center, MareNostrum's 9.96 Petaflop per second processing power solves some of the world's biggest problems:

Fighting cancer analyzing 20,000 genes and 500 tumors to correlate gene mutations with a particular type of cancer

Climate prediction analyzing variations in ocean temperatures over decades and seeking patterns between ocean temperatures and hurricanes such as Harvey to build future prediction models.

Designing smarter cities, crunching the data from a dozen European cities-- Stockholm, Cork, Cologne, Barcelona, etc. --- to develop strategies to manage future urban growth.

Quantum computing

Soon, even the most powerful super computers will be eclipsed by quantum computers. Powerful computer chips that can manipulate data using the principles of quantum physics, are ushering in the world of quantum computing, leaving even the most powerful supercomputers far behind. Google and IBM are both planning to have their commercial quantum chip ready for testing by the end of 2017 by early 2018.

Though it must be admitted that quantum computing is still in its infancy, it will be a sea change from classical computing. It is going to be the next great technological leap. It relies on the principles of quantum physics governing the behavior of subatomic particles such as electrons, protons, neutrons, and photons. Currently digital computers work on the principles of electricity and magnetism, electronics, and solid-state physics, and classical mechanics.

Quantum Bits (Qubits)

Prof Richard Feynman (1918-1988), theoretical physicist received the Nobel Prize in Physics in 1965 for his work in quantum electrodynamics. As mentioned by Paul Halpern in his book 'The Quantum Labyrinth' (2017), it was Prof Feynman who in a 1981 lecture had coined the term 'quantum computing'. The title of the lecture was

'Simulating Physics with Computers'. To reproduce the weirdness, the non-deterministic probabilistic nature of quantum mechanics, quantum computers had to be created in the place of digital computers that do linear processing of the two binary states.

The term quantum bits or qubits (attributed to Benjamin Schumacher) was coined based on quantum generalization of quantum bits. It considered the superposition of electron spin, or polarization states of photons.

Qubits and superposition

Digital computers use the binary system of 0 or 1 (electricity or magnetism on or off state). Quantum chips represent data using quantum bits or qubits in the place of binary digits or bits. Quantum computing uses quantum entities such as electrons, protons, neutrons, and photons that can be in two states (0 or 1) at the same time, referred to as '*superposition*'. This is the famous *Schrodinger cat paradox*, where the cat can be dead and alive at the same time. This is like parallel computing. Physical representation of qubits must be on an atomic scale, making use of a spin of an electron or the polarization of a photon.

Quantum computation relies on complex numbers rather than the real numbers 0 or 1. Complex numbers arose from solving equations such as $x^2+1=0$, when $x^2=-1$ or $x = \sqrt{(-1)}$.

Quantum entanglement

In addition to the principle of '*superposition*', quantum computers work on the principles of *quantum entanglement* for developing quantum memories. In entanglement, two or more quantum particles share a common state, for example: polarization of a photon horizontally or vertically. But each particle cannot be described independently.

Crystals doped with a rare element such as neodymium are used in quantum memories. A laser beam is fired at the crystal. This results in creation of pairs of entangled or correlated photons—photon one is entangled with photon two, meaning they have a fixed relationship. They have the same or opposite polarization when they are in superposition. A beam splitter sends the two entangled photons to different destinations. Photons polarized horizontally and vertically at the same time are super-positioned. Because they are entangled, observing photon one will influence photon 2, no matter how far apart they are. Their superposition will be lost, and each will appear either horizontally or vertically polarized.

Teleporting

Quantum theory and experiments prove that the quantum state of a pair of entangled (correlated) quantum particles can be teleported or carried from one location to another distant location. During the teleportation process, the particle at the sender's location will lose its quantum state, and it will be acquired by the particle at the receiver's location. This property allows quantum communication over large distances in space, using quantum repeaters. Quantum teleportation has been demonstrated between a satellite and a ground station in China over a distance covering around 1400 kilometers. Teleporting is helping to develop quantum communication systems and also quantum computer memory systems.

Computing power

Quantum computers have enormous computing power compared to today's binary computers. A quantum computer based on a 30-qubit processor would have the computing power of a conventional machine running at 10 teraflops (trillions of floating-point operations per second). It would be ten thousand times faster than conventional desktop computers today (measured in gigaflops or billions of floating-point operations per second).

Quantum processors need to be much larger than 50 qubits for useful work. It is challenging to build them as they require operations to be done on a subatomic scale. IBM's quantum computer, currently has 16 qubits. Google and IBM are both expecting to release 49-qubit or 50 qubit quantum computers by the end of 2017 or in 2018.

John Martinis is heading the 25-strong quantum computing research group at Google, building Google's quantum chip. The race is on between Intel, D-Wave, and IBM. Frontline research in this area is being led by Google, IBM, and Universities in USA, Singapore, Greece, Australia, Russia, China (Academy of Sciences), and Germany. Microsoft and Alibaba have also joined the Quantum Computing race.

Current state of quantum computing

Currently the Quantum Annealer (developed by D-Wave Systems, a Canadian company) has specialized architecture designed for optimization tasks. The next class would be the Analogue Quantum that may ultimately lead to the development of the Universal Quantum Computer. The Universal Quantum Computer could be described as a massively parallel processing machine.

Currently, the D-Wave 2X quantum computer of D-Wave Systems (Canada), has at its heart 1000 niobium loops, acting as the qubits. The 200 wires that connect the processor to the control electronics require to be heavily filtered to avoid interaction with the environment. The computer must be in a superconducting refrigeration system that cools the niobium loops to -273.13 degrees Celsius (0.015 Kelvin), that is 180 times colder than interstellar space. The quantum chip is magnetically shielded to 50,000 times less than the earth's magnetic field. The quantum computer has to be in a high vacuum environment to protect the supersensitive qubits. The internal pressure is maintained at 10 billion times lower than the atmospheric pressure.

That is a tall order. But the D-Wave 2X is 100 million times faster compared to an ordinary computer today. It can search simultaneously 2 raised to the power of 1000 solutions. Currently the greatest number of entangled qubits achieved is 1,000 (as against 100,000 qubits needed for a practical universal quantum computer. In the future (that may not be distant), a universal 64-qubit quantum computer could simultaneously perform 18.4 quintillion (i.e. 18.4×10^{18}) calculations!!

Because of the specialized cryogenic (super-cooled), high vacuum and controlled connectivity environments required for quantum computers, realizing desktop quantum computers may not be a possibility, at least in the near future. But classical computers could connect to quantum computers in the cloud. IBM has tried to make this a reality. The IBM Quantum Experience (www.ibm.com/ibmq) enables anyone to connect to IBM's experimental quantum computer hosted on the IBM Cloud. Users can deploy APIs to interface classical computers with IBM's five qubit cloud-based quantum computer, to run algorithms and experiments, and to explore simulations. This is still a primitive quantum computer but gives students and researchers an exposure to quantum computing and the enormous possibilities of the quantum age. Once developed, 'IBM Q' quantum systems and services will be delivered via the IBM Cloud Platform. In practical terms, a 5-qubit quantum machine is a toy, a 16-qubit machine would be useful for training. A 32-qubit would be the equivalent of a supercomputer. 32-qubit machines are expected to be available by 2022.

Applications of quantum computing

Quantum computing will revolutionize the world of computing, with the enormous processing power that will be unleashed. Quantum computers are expected to solve problems that take conventional computers longer than the lifetime of the universe to solve. They can design cryptosystems that are more secure than the existing ones.

Quantum computing will tackle highly complex problems that classical computing cannot solve easily. For example, examining the quantum states of a simple molecule like caffeine. Some of the areas where quantum computing is expected to make revolutionary changes are:

- Discovery of new drugs and materials (including nanomaterials)
- Supply Chain and Logistics: for determining optimal path across global systems for optimizing supplies and deliveries.
- Financial Services: Modeling financial data; identifying global risk factors for better investments.
- Artificial Intelligence: Designing machine algorithms for big data analytics and search algorithms for searching images or video, for example, improving facial recognition.
- Cloud Security: Using quantum physics to enhance privacy and security of data in the cloud.
- Space exploration: exploring the limits of the universe and communicating with alien beings in earthlike planets in other galaxies.
- Military intelligence and world security
- Enhanced encryption security.
- Bitcoin mining

Cloud Computing

Legacy data centers are now moving to the cloud. Improvements in and widespread adoption of virtual technologies and hypervisors, have led to the ushering in of on-demand computing from anywhere. These cloud servers and applications can be accessed from anywhere over the internet or on dedicated wide area network platforms. An era of utility computing like electricity as a utility, is emerging. Computing services are being offered by cloud service providers – Infrastructure as a Service (IaaS), Platform as a Service (PaaS), or Application as a Service (AaaS). Public cloud, private cloud or hybrid cloud services are being offered by cloud service providers such as IBM, HP, Google, Amazon (Amazon Web Services), Microsoft, RackSpace, Dell, etc.

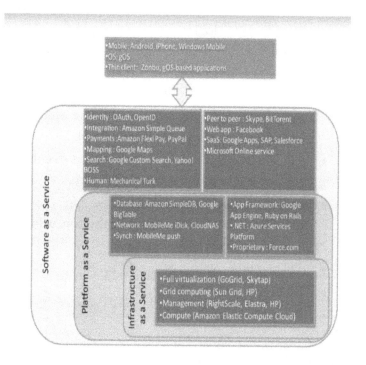

Fig. Courtesy: Cloud Security Alliance

Many cloud applications are now widely being used such as SalesForce.com, Gmail, Box, Dropbox, etc.

GE and Capital One, are two of the major enterprises that are closing their traditional data centers and moving their data centers to Amazon Web Service platform.

VMWare and Microsoft are two of the major players in the virtual technology arena.

Cloud Technology is driving enterprise collaboration. As reported by Forbes Magazine (July 27, 2017), Toyota, the Home Depot, and the Schneider Electric use the cloud content management and file sharing service Box to enable secure enterprise collaboration.

Three unicorns based in the 'Silicon Slopes' of Utah, namely Qualtrics (providing software to measure customer satisfaction and employee engagement), Domo (providing data analytics for customer data), and PluralSight (providing online corporate training), are leading cloud computing companies.

The main motivation for companies to migrate their applications to the cloud or to use cloud-based applications is the cost-savings from shutting down data centers. Symantec has moved its applications to Microsoft Azure, to cite a case in point.

What is cloud computing?

Cloud computing encompasses servers, networks, and data centers located or managed elsewhere (external to the enterprise) by Cloud Service Providers such as Microsoft, Amazon, Google, RackSpace, HP, IBM, and others.

It involves distributed computing services with multi-tenancy or many tenants or customers securely accessing and sharing the infrastructure and applications. The cloud service providers provide infrastructure (IaaS), platform (PaaS) and Software (SaaS) as services similar to utility services such as electricity or telephone. Amazon Web Services (AWS) was the first to enter the arena in 2006 with its Elastic Computer Cloud (EC2). Google AppEngine and Microsoft Azure followed suit.

Some of the most used enterprise cloud applications are Google Drive, Facebook, YouTube, Twitter, Google Gmail, iCloud (Apple Storage), Dropbox for storage, LinkedIn, Microsoft OneDrive (for storage), Box for storage and collaboration, Salesforce for CRM, Cisco WebEx for collaboration, Evernote for productivity, Microsoft Office 365 for collaboration, Pinterest, LivePerson (call center), HubSpot for marketing, Amazon CloudDrive for storage, Yammer (social networking), Concur for finance/accounting.

Today cloud applications are used in enterprises mostly for social networking and cloud storage.

The deployment models provide public, private, hybrid, or community cloud computing services. The service models cover infrastructure, platform, or software services. Cloud services provide resource pooling with broad network access, rapid elasticity, on-demand self-service, and measured service for utility billing.

In **Infrastructure Services**, *storage services* are provided by Amazon S3 & EBS, Rackspace Cloud Files, Nirvanix, AT&T Synaptic, and Zetta, to name a few.

Compute Services are provided by Amazon EC2, Serve Path GoGrid, Rackspace Cloud Servers, Joyent Cloud, Flexiant Flexiscale, Elastichosts, Terremark, iTRiCiTY, LayeredTech, Savvis Cloud Compute, Verizon CaaS,

AT&T Synaptic, Sungard Enterprise Cloud, Navisite.

Services Management is provided by Scair, CohesiveFT, Ylastic, CloudFounry, NewRelic, Cloud42, Amazon CloudWatch and Amazon VPC.

Under **Platform Services**, *general purpose services* are provided by force.com, Etelos, LongJump, Rollbase, Bungee Connect, Google App Engine, Engine Yard, Caspio, Qrimp, MS Azure, Mosso Cloud Sites, VMForce, Intuit Partner Platform, Joyent Smart Platform.

Business Intelligence Services are provided by Aster DB, Quantivo, Cloud9 Analytics, K2 Analytics, LogiXML, Oco, PivotLink, Clario Analytics, ColdLight Neuron, Vertica.

Integration Services are provided by Amazon SQS, Amazon SNS, Boomi, SnapLogic, IBM Cast Iron, gnip, Appian Anywhere, HubSpan, Informatica On-Demand.

Development & Testing Services are provided by Keynote Systems, SOASTA, SkyTap, Aptana, LoadStorm, Collabnet, Rational Software Delivery Services.

Database Service providers inlcude Amazon SimpleDB, Mosso Drizzle, Amazon RDS.

In **Cloud Software**, the major players are:

SaaS Data Security: Navajo, PerspecSys

Data: 10Gen, MongoDB, Apache CouchDb, Apache HBase, Hypertable, Tokyo Cabinet, Cassandra, memcached, Clustrix, FlockDb, Gizzard, Redis,

BerkeleyDB, Volernort, Terrastore.

Compute: Globus Toolkit, Xeround, Sun Grid Engine, Hadoop, OpenCloud, Gigaspaces, DataSynapse.

File Storage: EMC Atmos, ParaScale, Zmamda, CTERA, Appistry

Cloud Management: CA Turn-key Cloud, OpenNebula, Open.ControlTier, Enomaly Enomalism, VMware vCloud, CohesiveFT VPN Cubed, Hyperic, Eucalyptus, Puppet Labs, Appistry, IBM CloudBurst, CISCO UCS, Zenoss, Surgient.

In the **Software Services** space, we have several players:

Financials: Concur, Zero, Workday, Expensify, Intuit Quickbooks Online.

Content Management: Clickability, SpringCM, CrownPoint.

Collaboration: Box.net, CubeTree, SocialTexst, Basecamp, Assembla, DropBox

Social Networks: Ning, Zembly, Arnitive, Jive SBS

Sales: Xactly, StreetSmarts, Success Metrics

Desktop Productivity: Zoho, Google Apps, HyerOffice, MS Office Web Apps

CRM: NetSuite, Parature, Responsys, Rightnow, LiveOps, MSDynamics, Salesforce.com, Oracle On Demand

Document Management: NetDocuments, DocLanding, Knowlege TreeLive, SpringCM

Virtualization

The Cloud architecture relies on virtualization provided by the hypervisors (such as VMWare, Xen, KVM or Hyper-V) sharing the host operating system and the shared physical hardware. The hypervisors running on the host operating system enable several virtual machines that can run different operating systems. The applications are controlled by the virtual machines.

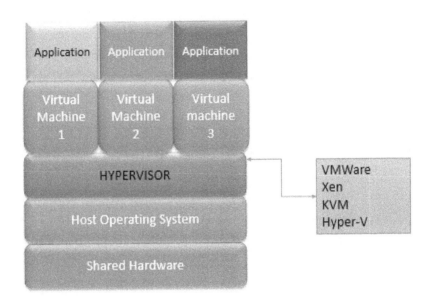

Fig. Virtual Systems in Cloud Architecture

Edge Computing /Fog Computing

Because of the overheads of virtualization, cloud computing has the drawback of communication and network bandwidth latency, impacting performance. Cloud services required by Internet of Things (IoT) described below, have created the need for edge computing. In edge computing, data processing occurs in part at the network edge, rather than completely in the cloud. With massive amounts of data being generated by IoT devices, network will be bottleneck for cloud computing and hence the need for edge computing devices.

WAN Connectivity

Wide Area Network (WAN) connectivity will continue to use improved satellite communication systems, optical fiber networks coaxial cable systems, virtual private networks (VPN), frame relay and MPLS (Multi-Protocol Label Switching) connectivity. AT&T, Verizon, and other telecommunication carrier networks are improving their systems to meet the high bandwidth requirements of a massively connected world. These communication systems will have to meet the increasing demands for telephony, data, and audio-video conferencing requirements.

Digital Silk Road

BeiDou (Chinese name for 'Big Dipper) is China's answer to rival America's Global Positioning System (GPS). As reported in the Economist (The World in 2018), China is extending coverage of its satellite-navigation system (with a network of 35 satellites) to around 60 countries covering the old Silk Road region, calling it the Silk Road Economic Belt. China will be building the ground stations and improving the information infrastructure in these regions, laying fiber-optic cables for high-speed internet. The coverage will extend from Xian in China to Tehran, Istanbul, Moscow, Rotterdam, Venice, Athens, Mombasa, Hambantota (Sri Lanka), Kolkata, Kuala Lumpur, Zhanjiang, and Fuzhou.

Currently around 150 million Chinese smartphones are equipped with BeiDou. Fishing vessels, bicycles, and motorcycles use it to communicate. BeiDou system controlled by Chinese military will be the fourth global navigational system in the world, the other three being managed by Europe, America, and Russia.

Mobile & Communication Technologies

Wired Ethernet connectivity for telephone, data and digital TV is moving from coaxial cable connectivity to optical fiber networks. Improved wireless network connectivity will be required by sensor networks for IoT devices and smart phone networks.

With increased use of IoT devices, Machine to Machine (M2M) connectivity will be an important feature of the emerging world. With 50 billion internet of things devices being connected by 2020, the challenges are felt by communication technologies and providers.

We are already seeing the introduction of 5G smart phones. Smart phone capabilities are now being enhanced with voice recognition systems and virtual reality (VR) and augmented reality (AR) features.

Connecting the unconnected world is still a major

challenge. Facebook, Google, and major carriers are working in this area.

5G

Around 40% of the world population today has an internet connection over connectivity provided by coaxial cable or optical fiber or cellular wireless (CDMA, TDMA, or GSM) networks. This enables online accessibility in rural and remote areas. The fourth generation or 4G wireless connectivity is still being implemented in many countries. There is demand for faster and more reliable networks with increasing growth in data traffic that includes streaming video traffic. The telecommunications industry is now moving towards implementing 5G networks that are expected to provide connection speeds up to 10 gigabits per second (Gbps). 5G networks would be required to connect the estimated 50 billion IoT devices by 2020.

Li-Fi vs. Wi-Fi

Prof. Harald Haas of the University of Edinburgh, in a 2011 TED Talk, introduced Light Fidelity or Li-Fi using light signals (including infrared and ultraviolet light waves) as a speedier alternative to Wi-Fi that uses radio signal to communicate data. Wi-Fi has limited frequency range as the radio frequency spectrum limits its capacity. The TV remote uses infra-red-light pulses to send signals. Li-Fi is an evolution from infra-red signal and Bluetooth omnidirectional signal communication.

Li-Fi can fit more data into its signal than Wi-Fi. The visible light range of the electromagnetic spectrum is 10,000 times bigger than the entire radio spectrum. Wi-Fi, on the other hand, is restricted to a tiny portion of the radio spectrum.

Li-Fi has reached speeds of 224 gigabits per second (as against the 100 megabits per second (Mbps) speeds currently available in 4G mobile networks or the 10 Gbps expected in 5G wireless networks). Li-Fi can use LED (light-emitting diode) bulbs used in homes as Li-Fi routers. Li-Fi has the additional advantage that it is not subject to electromagnetic interference to which Wi-Fi radio waves are subject to. However, Li-Fi cannot penetrate walls, unlike radio waves. This limits the range of Li-Fi, though it makes it more secure than Wi-Fi, and also protects communication privacy.

Pure Li-Fi, the company promoted by Prof Harald Hass and the Li-Fi consortium are working to make the technology commercially viable. Dubai in UAE is planning to fit its street lights with Li-Fi.

Li-Fi use will be restricted to home or office to connect devices. It will not replace mobile phone technologies like 4G or the microwave wireless links used to connect buildings.

Li-Fi-enabled LED bulbs, mounted on a ceiling, are wired to the Ethernet port to connect to the Internet. A simple USB dongle can connect any computer to the Li-Fi network.

Chapter 4

THE SMART WORLD -- INTERNET OF THINGS (IoT)

Internet is evolving from connecting people to connecting devices (things) with which people interact. Brue Sinclair in *'IOT Inc-How Your Company can Use the Internet of Things to Win in the Outcome Economy'* describes how the Internet is extending its reach to physical objects. Internet of Things (IoT) is now connecting devices across the spectrum from consumers to commercial users, manufacturing and infrastructure objects. Internet of Things will impact human life in all its aspects – healthcare, education, energy, transportation and even food. The Internet will be interwoven or integrated into everything that we do. Machine-to-Machine (M2M) connectivity is giving rise to 'the smarts'- smart cities, smart grids, smart transportation systems, smart cars, smart devices. According to Goldman Sachs, the business of connected devices is increasing at a rapid rate providing enormous business opportunities.

Machine to machine networks and Internet of Things (IoT) for connected devices have been in development since 1999 for automated supply chain management. Computers automatically detect and process sensor information without human intervention. This concept is now applied to fields such as healthcare, home technology, environmental engineering, and transportation. The sensors attached to these devices generate massive data. Applications deployed at the network edge will have to process such massive information.

It is estimated by CISCO Systems that by 2020 there will be 50 billion devices connected to the Internet. These include computers (desktops, notebooks, tablets), smart-phones, webcams, copy machines, printers, home appliances such as TV, fridge, car, coffee makers, wearables (iglass, iwatch) and medical devices such as pacemakers.

GE, CISCO, IBM, Samsung, and Google are focusing on IoT business. Samsung acquired SmartThings. Google also acquired NEST (known for their thermostat and smoke detectors). Apple's iWatch can be used for monitoring health of individuals.

San Diego's Streetlight IoT Network

3200 smart streetlights will be used by the City of San Diego not only to light up the streets, but to spot parking spaces, spot illegally parked cars, monitor for safety incidents, and track air pollution or other environmental parameters. Each IoT streetlight designed and operated by Current, a subsidiary of General Electric, includes an Intel Atom processor, 0.5 TB of memory, Bluetooth and Wi-Fi radios, two 1080p video cameras for video, still images, and computer vision analytics, two acoustical sensors, and environmental sensors to monitor temperature, pressure,

107

humidity, vibration, and magnetic fields. Much of the data will be processed on board, but selected events and data streams will be uploaded to GE's Predix cloud through AT&T's LTE network. Each sensing light will monitor an oval area roughly 120 to 180 feet. (IEEE Spectrum, January 2018, *'San Diego's Streetlights Get Smart'*). In addition to this, San Diego will be replacing an additional 14,000 of the city's streetlights with energy-efficient LED lamps that can communicate with each other.

GE is replicating the San Diego experience to other cities such as Atlanta, Singapore, London, Chicago, Chongqing (China).

Consumer IoT – Smart Homes & Smart Appliances

Connected devices for the consumer can transform dumb homes into smart homes covering security, health, home economics, and energy management. Smart home and personal products such as smart appliances, beds, smart wear, cars, and even smart toothbrushes, are entering the market. IoT will power driverless cars. Wearables can help to manage and prevent disease, by monitoring the health condition of the wearer.

Commercial IoT

Commercial IoT and connected devices will transform every industry. In transportation, IoT-enabled trucks can be used for fleet management with telematics.

IoT-enabled equipment can be monitored for safety and efficient use. Every commercial equipment and device currently used can be reengineered and fitted with sensors and transmitters to capture and relay relevant data for monitoring.

Industrial IoT

IoT-enabled and connected devices will make manufacturing smarter. In the oil and gas industries, sensor data analysis can lead to more efficient oil and gas extraction, processing, and supply. In mining, autonomous and safe equipment can be monitored 24 x 7. In agriculture, crop sensors and environmental data services can be used for crop yield monitoring augmented by machine learning to increase output.

Infrastructure IoT

Infrastructure services will be impacted by IoT sensors. Smart cities will monitor traffic movement and vehicle safety, and more efficient routing of traffic. Utilities will use smart grids and smart meters for more efficient distribution of power.

IoT is enabling a shift of business from product and service orientation of the economy to networking of products and services to create the outcomes desired by customers. Bruce Sinclair calls it an *'Outcome Economy'*.

Object identification

All physical objects on the Internet will be identified by their IP address. Currently IPv6 is used. Objects can also be identified by their RFID (Radio Frequency Identification System) that can transmit their IDs using the RF transmitter. RFID will replace the UPC (Universal

Product Code) currently used to identify merchandise.

Sensor Technology

As pointed out by Paul Saffo, technology forecaster and associate professor at Stanford University, processors, networking, and sensors define the digital revolution. First, we created the processors and computers, networked and internetworked them, and now we are giving them the sensory organs to observe.

IoT Technology is based on sensors and actuators and the communication systems. IoT devices will have embedded microprocessors and communication systems.

Sensors and actuators act as a digital nervous system. These may include GPS sensors, cameras, microphones, or sensors to measure temperature, pressure, electric/magnetic fields, acoustics/sound/vibration, or force/load/torque, sensors to detect gas and chemicals, or flow meters to detect flow levels or leaks.

Some of the sensors that we use in daily life are:

- Temperature sensor in a microwave
- Temperature and humidity sensors in an AC
- Smoke detectors and fire alarm
- Tire pressure sensors
- Detection sensors in an ATM (automated teller machines)
- Photoelectric sensors used for closing and opening garage doors
- Capacitor sensors used on conveyor belts to

examine the contents of dielectric materials such as glass, plastics, liquid, etc.

- Induction sensors used in automated lifts.

In industrial control systems, sensors play a major role. Process automation sensors measure temperature, pressure, liquid level and flow, humidity, viscosity, pH, chemical parameters, etc.

Factory automation sensors may use electro-magnetic induction, capacitors, ultrasonic sensors, photoelectric sensors, transformers, position sensors, etc.

Sensor technology is helping us to make advances in astronomy. Today robotic systems to detect signals across the electromagnetic spectrum are used for astronomical discoveries.

Intelligent Network Infrastructure for IoT

For IoT devices to perform effectively, there must be continuous connectivity. The network infrastructure must rely on wired and wireless networks connecting the devices and facilitating the data transfer to the data centers. The sensors and network switches, and the network connectivity and bandwidth, and security, are key factors determining the success of IoT networks. It would require intelligent networks with built-in analytics, to determine efficient routing and to optimize the network functions.

There will be millions of endpoints, such as watches, door locks, refrigerators, smart shoes, smart glasses, and smart apparels. If they have not been configured securely, they could pose security threats to the whole IoT network and infrastructure. IoT network and endpoint security would be crucial in such scenarios. Added to all this is the requirement that IoT demands 100% availability, and failure is not an option.

IoT Connectivity & Communication

The inputs are digitized and transmitted over the networks.

The communication networks include PAN (Personal Area Network), LAN (Local Area Network), MAN (Metropolitan Area Network) or Wide Area Network, or the Inter-Planetary Network.

The communication protocols used could include Ethernet, RFID, ANT, NFC, 6LoWPAN, ZIGBEE, Z-WAVE, UWB, Bluetooth, WiFi, Internet Protocols IPv4, IPv6, UDP, DTLS, RPL, Telnet, MQTT, DDS, CoAP, XMPP, HTTP, SOCKETS or REST API.

Many of the SCADA systems used for Industrial Control use proprietary communication protocols such as MODBUS.

Communication Technologies used in sensor networks include LTE Advanced, Cellular 4G/LTE, 5G, 3G-GPS/GPRS, GSM, EDGE, CDMA, EVDO, WEIGHTLESS, WIMAX, License-free spectrum, DASH7.

The device IDs, sensors, and communication protocols help to track, control, and manage the physical objects (machines, appliances, buildings, vehicles, animals, plants).

IoT Networks

IoT Gateway will connect to the IoT sensors, gather data and forward the data to the cloud or to the fog / edge for processing and action.

For short ranges WPAN (Wireless Personal Area Networks) using the ZigBee (802.15.4 protocol), Bluetooth or NFC protocols can also be used.

For Long Ranges, Low Power LPWAN networks are used. LoRA is a proprietary protocol used for that purpose.

Long Range RF networks

Long Range RF networks facilitate remote monitoring and communication with IoT devices.

LoRa is the Long Range, low power wireless platform technology for IoT sensor networks. This employs wireless RF technology that can be integrated into cars, street lights, manufacturing equipment, home appliances, wearable devices, etc.

It provides greater range coverage than cellular networks.

LPWAN (Low Power WAN)

LoRaWAN is the protocol specification built on top of the LoRa technology developed by the LoRa Alliance. It uses unlicensed radio spectrum in the Industrial, Scientific, and Medical (ISM) bands, enabling low power, wide area communication between remote sensors and gateways.

THE SMART WORLD --INTERNET OF THINGS (IoT)

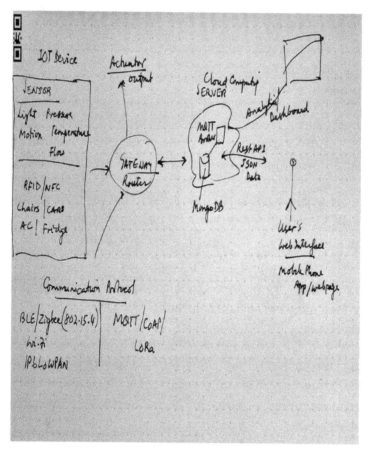

The IoT devices will connect to the Concentrator or Gateway using the LoRa RF LoRaWAN open protocol. The concentrator will then connect over TCP/IP SSL to the Network Server and then to the application server, mostly in the cloud. Microsoft provides the Azure IoT Hub for connecting to IoT devices and then further processing the IoT data.

The application payload traffic could be encrypted using AES.

Semtech IoT chip provides the wireless modulation for the long-range communication link through the LoRa-enabled modem and antenna. The LoRa RF transceivers (of Semtech) are embedded into the sensors. The Picocells and Gateways capture and transmit the data over a long range.

A base station can connect to 30 miles away. Embedded end-to-end AES128 encryption of traffic makes the connectivity secure.

CISCO IoT network architecture

Traditional IP networks have limitations to cater to the requirements of IoT networks to analyze traffic from millions of connected devices. The bandwidth and error rates of IP networks do not make them suitable for IoT networks.

CISCO's architectural approach is

1. Embedded systems and sensors will use smart things network (wired or wireless). End Points (Smart Water meters, Structural Health, Intelligent Transportation, Public Lighting, Environmental Monitoring, Safety & Security) will connect to the CISCO Router over WiFi, 802.11P, Wave2M, Low Power RF, PLC, 802.15.4, Ethernet, etc.
2. Multi-Service Edge connectivity of 3G /4G /LTE /WiFi /Ethernet /PLC will use the Field Area Network for computing and storage
3. Core Networking Services (IP/MPLS, QoS, Multicast) will use IP/MPLS Core and Cloud/Fog computing.

115

THE SMART WORLD --INTERNET OF THINGS (IoT)

IoT Protocols supported by CISCO are:

- IEEE 802.15.4 sub-GHz RF Mesh
- 6LoWPAN
- Routing RPL
- CoAP (Constrained Application Protocol: RFC 7252)

CISCO also employs Self Learning Networks by embedding predictive analytics into data gathered to manage networks.

IoT Data Analytics & Security

Capturing the massive data from the connected devices and analyzing them in a timely and efficient manner is important for making IoT systems efficient and effective. The main challenges that IoT will face include, identifying security and privacy risks, and implementing adequate security safeguards to protect privacy information and to protect the devices, the networks, and the data transmitted and stored. Big Data-driven analysis is helping in urban planning.

Smart Cities

An increasing proportion of the world's population lives in cities--- 3.42 billion in urban areas as against 3.45 billion people in rural areas, as of mid-2009, according to the United Nations estimate. As a result, services such as public transportation, energy provisioning, or the urban road network are strained. Emerging technologies can help to make cities greener.

The concept of smart cities has arisen from the fact that an increasingly urbanized world is dealing with scarce resources leading to the need for improving energy efficiency. There is traffic congestion on the roads leading to loss of human efficiency and productivity and also waste of scarce energy resources. The stressed civic resources must be allocated more efficiently. Overall there is need to improve the quality of life.

Smarter solutions can be deployed to lessen the negative effects of growing urbanization. Sensors can be used to monitor traffic. Smarter ticketing solutions can be implemented by traffic police without holding up traffic. Smart cities will have multiple arrays of tiny, low-power sensors and transmitters to remain connected using Wi-Fi or LoRa connectivity.

Promotion of electric vehicles can reduce pollution. For areas of the world where water is a scarce resource, smart cities can allocate this precious resource using sensors to provide critical information on water-storage levels. Light-Emitting Diodes (LEDs) and solar cells can reduce the costs of street-lighting, an area that can take as much as 40 per cent of a city's energy budget.

There are also other benefits of creating smart cities. They can generate new remote employment opportunities, reducing the need for citizens to be physically present in their places of work. Improvement in quality of life can help to reduce costs of transportation, utility and energy and even health-care.

THE SMART WORLD --INTERNET OF THINGS (IoT)

Futuristic Cities

Santander (Spain), Boston, MA (USA), Singapore, Seoul (South Korea), Nairobi (Kenya), and Masdar City (UAE, are emerging as model 'smart cities'.

The city of Santander in Northern Spain uses tens of thousands of sensors to connect buildings, infrastructure, traffic, networks, and utilities. The sensors monitor the levels of pollution, noise, traffic, and parking. Smart cards with a unique encrypted identifier, carried by a person, allows the person to log in to a range of government-provided services (or e-services) without setting up multiple accounts. The single identifier allows governments to aggregate data about citizens and their preferences to improve the provision of services and to determine common interests of groups. Soil humidity sensors detect when land requires irrigation for more sustainable water use.

Singapore has implemented smart water supply system. Sensors embedded on the water pipes constantly measure and monitor pressure and water flow, and identity leaks. Singapore, the 'garden city', implemented a sustainable city garden in 2011, covering 101 hectares of parkland. Singapore has become a model for recycling. It collects rainwater, harvests sunlight, uses decaying plants and waste as fertilizer and as energy source. 18 super-trees house almost 163,000 plants. The environmentally-controlled glass houses contain numerous plant species. Rainwater that is harvested is used to irrigate the gardens.

Newark, USA has indoor farms growing leafy greens and herbs in vertical farming. Light of varying wavelengths is used to boost the crop yield, optimizing the use of water. In the future, city skyscrapers will be surrounded by vertical farms growing food crops.

Berlin, Germany is prototyping a flexible film to harvest solar energy. The film can be installed on building façade or outer surface of buildings.

Smart bins powered by a solar panel and internet-enabled, are used in many cities and towns to compress waste and to alert collectors when full. They can also be used as Wi-Fi hotspots.

Public parks and rooftop gardens will drain storm water. Rooftop water tanks and solar panels will capture heat and light from the sun.

Mega tunnels enabling rail and road networks to run underground, alongside smart utilities (water and solid waste). Solid waste can be transformed into vehicle fuel and electricity.

Masdar City (UAE) is a futuristic city being built on the outskirts of Abu Dhabi in UAE. The plans unveiled in 2008 to house 50,000 residents, included a car-free transport system relying on driverless pods running on magnetic tracks, energy harvesting technologies in every home, and 'net zero' carbon and waste.

The homes and buildings use solar energy for electricity needs and for hot water supply. For transportation, as implemented electric cars are taking precedence over driverless pods. The city is still under construction.

Songdo (South Korea) with a current population of

100,000 is another leader in use of smart technologies. In the pneumatic waste disposal system, all waste is managed underground. Sensors detect whether the bin is full and then the waste is automatically sucked through vacuum tubes to a central processing facility. Food waste gets transformed into compost for city parks, while recyclable waste is cleaned and processed for recycling.

Challenges ahead for urban planning

Some of the major challenges to be tackled in urban planning are:

- Waste management
- Traffic management
- Energy
- Air pollution
- Water desalination
- Increasing housing demand
- Dealing with plastic waste and e-waste
- Noise pollution
- Ageing population and their physical challenges such as loss of vision, hearing loss, and physical impairment.

Transportation

The auto industry is being disrupted by ride-hailing smartphone applications such as Uber, Ola, and Lyft. Ola is India's ride hailing service. These companies do not own any vehicles. The question being asked is 'why drive when I can ride'. It questions the need to own a vehicle. The Economist has highlighted this trend in their video series

'Disrupters'.

Car manufacturers such as Ford are trying out new business models with decreasing trend for ownership of vehicles and trying out shared transport.

In the world of transportation, some of the initiatives of Elon Musk that will further disrupt the transportation industry are Tesla (electric car), Space X (for inter-planetary travel), Hyperloop (high-speed transportation using a vacuum tube), and Boring Company for underground tunnel transportation to relieve city traffic congestion. SpaceX has successfully tested Falcon 9 reusable rockets that are currently being used by NASA for transporting cargo from and to the International Space Station.

Elon Musk's vision is to use SpaceX to create passenger rockets to travel to any city in the world in less than an hour for 'earth-to-earth' travel. He plans to build a permanent moon base and send humans to Mars in the next decade.

Autonomous Vehicles

Driverless cars or autonomous vehicles driven by sensors and machine learning algorithms are already a reality. Companies such as Alphabet (Google), Uber, Toyota, Nissan, BMW, Ford, are already working in this field. Baidu, the Chinese search engine company has also invested in this area. Automakers Ford and BMW are expecting to have autonomous cars on the road by 2021.

A key element in these vehicles is the lidar (light detection and ranging) sensor required to map objects in 3-D, sending and receiving back laser beams from surrounding objects. The world's leading lidar sensor manufacturer is Velodyne. Quanergy, a startup, is also developing solid-state sensors that are cheaper.

Tesla instead of relying on lidar sensors is using cameras and radar using microwave and ultrasonic sensors.

Drones & Flying Taxis

Drones are flying objects that can be remotely controlled using a RC transmitter. Hi-tech drones have been used by the military for unmanned aerial operations. But now we are seeing smaller drones being put to commercial use. Amazon and Google have started using drones for physical delivery of packages.

Commercial drones are now being employed in real estate, monitoring construction sites, golfing, aerial inspections, agriculture, security, search and rescue operations, package delivery, land surveying, cinematography, or insurance claims. NASA, the National Oceanic and Atmospheric Administration (NOAA), and Northrop Grumman (a global security company) teamed up to use Unmanned Aerial Vehicles (UAV) for monitoring storms as they evolve. In Japan, drones are used in agriculture to monitor crops and to control application of pesticides, water, and fertilizers. Drones are also used in wildlife conservation efforts in Indonesia and Malaysia.

Drones can be Wi-Fi-enabled so that they can beam videos and images to a smart phone, tablet or computer. Wi-Fi can be used to remotely control the drone. Most remote-control drones use 900 MHz radio frequency for signal transmission, while those which are Wi-Fi-enabled use higher frequencies in the 2.4 GHz range. Drones using ultra-high radio frequencies have a limited range up to 600 meters.

Uber has a project to develop flying taxis, in collaboration with Carnegie Mellon University.

In smart cities, unmanned drones could deliver medicines, groceries, and parcels to homes, or designated collection spots. This could reduce city traffic.

In Africa, drones are used to deliver medicines and essential supplies in areas that are not easily reachable because of the terrain or because of lack of navigable roads.

Chapter 5

LIVING WITH INTELLIGENT MACHINES

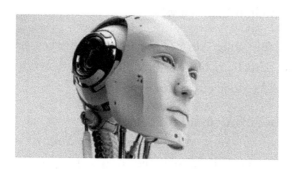

Artificial Intelligence

It was in 1996 that IBM's DeepBlue defeated Chess Grandmaster Garry Kasparov for the first time. Garry Kasparov, in 'Deep Thinking –Where Machine Intelligence Ends and Human Creativity Begins' (2017) has explained in detail his encounter with the Deep Blue.

In 2011, IBM Watson defeated the Jeopardy champions Ken Jennings and Brad Rutter. In March 2016, Google's AlphaGo defeated Lee Sedol, the world's Go Champion. In all these cases, computers powered by artificial intelligence using deep learning algorithms, outperformed their human opponents in these highly skilled games involving natural language processing, information retrieval, automated reasoning, and machine learning.

From robotic surgery to using robots on the shop-floor

and even in restaurants, robots are replacing humans in repetitive mechanical tasks and even in dangerous situations. A robot, normally used for defusing bombs, was used to kill a terrorist sniper who shot and killed five police officers in Dallas, TX. Robots are used extensively by Amazon in their fulfillment centers. Future wars will be in cyberspace and on the ground robotic armies will replace the human army for most purposes. In the air, unmanned robot-controlled or remote-controlled drones will carry lethal weapons into enemy territory. These raise concerns of safety and survival of humankind in the future.

On the positive front, problem solving based on Artificial Intelligence (AI) and other digital technologies may lead to replacement of professionals such as doctors, lawyers, and other professionals. AI is moving beyond the realm of just duplicating human reasoning and thinking. Machine Learning and Deep Learning are outpacing the limits of human reasoning and thinking. With the increasing use of AI and machine learning, the role of humans will shift more to areas that require judgment, creativity, empathy, and collaboration, while using these techniques to enhance human capacity.

In his annual letter to shareholders in April 2017, Amazon CEO Jeff Bezos noted that AI will be the key technology that will drive Amazon's future. AI is already a part of the Amazon DNA driving many of its major services: autonomous Prime Air delivery drones, Amazon Go convenience store, and Amazon Alexa voice assistant. Amazon Web Services (AWS), Amazon's cloud computing platform incorporates deep learning features such as Lex, Polly, and Rekognition. Today AWS is offering AI/deep learning/ machine learning as a service.

Natural language processing, voice recognition, and computer vision will drive consumer internet in the coming years, according to Barclays. Andrew Ng, former Chief Scientist at Baidu, compared AI to the advent of electricity. According to him AI will transform every industry in the near future.

Digital Virtual Assistants

The digital virtual assistants Apple SIRI, Amazon Echo, Google Home, and Microsoft's Cortana --all rely on Artificial Intelligence (AI) technology, particularly speech recognition systems.

Apple included SIRI, the virtual assistant, in its iPhones in 2011. In 2014 Amazon came out with its Echo, a speaker with speech recognition technology Alexa.

Virtual assistant platforms can be a launching pad to connect to other services. You can ask Alexa for the weather and news, ask it to play music or a video, show photographs, ask for information on any subject, and connect over telephone to your friends or family members. It can also enable video telephony. Alexa also can connect you to your IoT devices. Through the virtual assistant you can control the temperature, open or close the garage door, check food in the fridge, and so on.

Robotic Soldiers

By 2010, the US Army had deployed a fleet of about 3000 small tactical robots to detect and disable improvised explosive devices on exposed roads or dark caves. This fleet was composed of iRobot's PackBot and QinetiQ Talon. These robotic soldiers have jointed arms fitted with video cameras surveying their surroundings and having claws to pick up or examine explosive devices. They are not autonomous but remotely controlled like toy cars. PackBot is almost similar to iRobot's Roomba, the robotic vacuum cleaner.

Artificial Emotional Intelligence

In MIT Technology Review Vol 120, No. 6 November/December 2017, Rana el Kaliouby, CEO and Co-founder of Affectiva, in 'We Need Computers with Empathy', writes about an emerging category of AI – artificial emotional intelligence or emotion AI. Her company Affectiva has compiled data of six million face videos from 87 countries for analysis by an AI engine to identify human emotions of happiness, sadness, anger and cognitive states of fatigue, attention, interest, confusion, distraction, etc. taking into consideration cultural differences. The challenge is in capturing less frequent emotions such as pride or inspiration. The goal is to develop emotion-aware AI machines that could sense and respond to the emotional state of humans. If it finds that you are stressed, it could adjust the lighting and turn on a mood-enhancing music. It uses computer vision, speech analysis, and deep learning to classify facial and vocal expressions of emotion.

Some of the application areas are listed below:

Automotive: The system could monitor the driver for fatigue, distraction, or frustration. It could create safety alert, or change the music or ergonomic settings.

Education: Intelligent learning systems could sense whether the student is frustrated, confused, and struggling, and could provide a personalized learning experience.

Healthcare: To track the mental state of a patient, and to perform early diagnosis of diseases such as Parkinson's, coronary artery disease, and to provide suicide prevention and autism support.

Communication: Providing emotional and moral support to those physically abused, those suffering from illness, and to help youngsters develop empathy. Today's youngsters spend their time with machines that lack emotions. Emotional AI machines could fill that gap.

The downside is that these devices can cross privacy and moral or ethical boundaries. They must have built-in controls and safeguards to protect privacy and to conform to ethical guidelines.

Robots That Feel

If emotion and intelligence are inextricably linked and emotions affect intelligence, and vice versa, can robots without emotions be effective in autonomous situations, as in a battlefield? This issue is discussed by Louisa Hall in MIT Technological Review in 'How We Feel About Robots That Feel?'

Octavia is a humanoid robot created by the US Navy Center for Applied Research in Artificial Intelligence. She is designed to fight fires on Navy ships and is also designed to 'think and act in ways like people'. She displays an impressive range of emotions as facial expressions while interacting with humans—looking pleased, surprised, confused, and so on. She has massive amounts of information about her environment. She has two cameras built into her eyes to analyze characteristics such as facial features, complexion, and clothing of those around. She can detect people's voices using four microphones and a voice recognition program called Sphinx. She can identify 25 different objects by touch. The perceptual skills form part of her 'embodied cognitive architecture'.

Pepper is a 'pleasant and likeable' humanoid built by SoftBank Robotics, to serve as a human companion. Pepper can perceive human emotions and respond with happy smiles or sad expressions. But the makers do not claim that Pepper 'feels' such emotions as humans.

The difficulty in capturing and encoding human emotions is that they vary depending on human cultures and even in different situations. It is currently difficult to model human emotions in robots.

Can robot write a symphony? Shimon is a robot developed by Georgia Tech's Center for Music Technology. It can compose and play music. It is fed with music of all composers from Beethoven to Lady Gaga. It uses deep learning technology.

Robotics

Developments in robotics were fueled by the need for applications in space exploration such as robotic arms, and robotic rovers to explore the surface of the moon and Mars. Robotic tanks also found deployment in military operations. Today robotic manufacturing systems, robotic surgery systems, and robots on the shop floor of Amazon fulfillment centers, or even robots doing assembling and painting in car manufacturing plants have become common. Robotic chef and robotic kitchens have appeared in Japan.

Soon we will be seeing robots powered by expert systems replacing professional services of physicians, nurses, and even engineers and accountants. A robot adviser on the corporate boards of directors will soon be reality.

At the corporate level, Google has been in the forefront of robotic and AI development. Google's acquisition of Boston Dynamics and DeepMind pointed to the importance that Google has attached to Artificial Intelligence and robotics research and development. Google also invested heavily in the robocar or autonomous cars. Amazon also is deploying robots on the shop floor of its fulfillment centers, and also developing and deploying the airborne delivery drones and automated delivery trucks.

At the government level, in 2011 US President Obama launched the *National Robotics Initiative* under the National Science Foundation to stimulate use of robots in industrial automation, military applications, and in care of the elderly population.

Alec Ross in his book *'The Industries of the Future'* (2016) describes how in the future humans will have to live alongside robots. Labor shortage in Japan makes robots a necessity. Japan's aging population requiring eldercare turn to robots as future caretakers. Toyota and Honda, leveraging their expertise in mechanical engineering, are building the next generation of robots. Toyota built the robot *Robina*, as a nursing aide. Robina's brother *Humanoid* is a multi-purpose human assistant, washing dishes, taking care of sick persons, providing entertainment playing the violin or playing the trumpet.

Honda created ASIMO (the Advanced Step in Innovative Mobility Robot) that can interpret human emotions, movements, and conversation. ASIMO's computer vision capability and voice recognition systems and mechanical parts can interpret voice commands, shake hands, and answer questions with a nod or by voice. He bows to greet people, following Japanese manners. He helps elderly people to get out of bed or to have a conversation. Honda is focusing on research on robotic limbs and robotic assistance devices, to help paraplegics walk.

AIST, a Japanese industrial automation company, is focusing on robotic pets. PARO is a robot baby harp seal covered in soft white fur, exhibiting many of the behaviors of a real pet.

According to Alec Ross, Japan leads the world in robotics, operating 310,000 of the 1.4 million industrial robots in the world, as in 2016. The big five in robotics are Japan, China, US, South Korea, and Germany. Japan, the United States, and Germany focus on high-value industrial and medical robots. South Korea and China are major producers of consumer-oriented robots. Russia is almost a non-player in robotics as it focuses on natural gas, oil, and mineral extraction industries. Robots are fast moving from the manufacturing sector to consumer and service sector.

Robots are entering areas that require situational awareness, spatial reasoning and dexterity, and human judgment. Advances in data mining and analytics, and machine learning, are enabling robots to interact intelligently with their environment.

Cloud robotics has been popularized by James Kuffner of Google since 2010 and involves networked robotic devices linked to the cloud and accessing vast data stores (mostly unstructured data) enabling robots to have more intelligence and shared experience of other robotic devices operating in similar environments. Big Data analytics is enabling cognitive computing by machines.

How do robots work?

The sensor circuitry captures the input from computer vision systems, voice recognition, sensors measuring temperature or pressure, Radio Frequency (RF) signals, or GPS (Global Positioning System) location information, or a combination of these and other parameters captured by sensors.

The sensor inputs are processed by CPU (Central Processing Unit) powered by powerful microprocessors (embedded systems) and GPUs (Graphical Processing Units). The computer circuitry, Programming Logic Controllers (PLCs), data acquisition systems, industrial control systems / SCADA are part of the processing system.

The processor systems are controlled by the AI software and machine learning algorithms that are designed for specific robotic use cases.

The output from the robotic system consists of the electro-mechanical systems of actuator motors, relays, and robotic arms. Advances in material science and nanotechnology have helped to build the outer bodies of robots that are as flexible as human limbs and muscular systems.

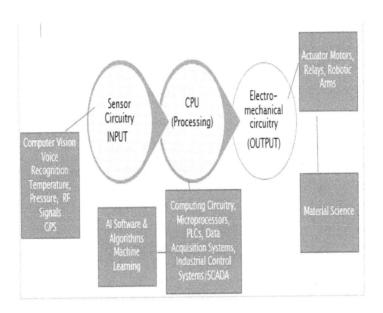

Industrial Robots

90% of the robots in the world today are in factories, particularly in areas where it is not safe for humans to work.

General Motors was the first to install an industrial robot in 1961. Its Unimate, a 1.8 ton, robot arm handled red-hot, metal car door handles and other auto parts. The instructions or programs were stored on a magnetic drum (similar to hard disks). Later it took over the job of welding car bodies in 1969. This led to increased production of cars.

Intelligent vs. Conscious Machines

Robots are gradually moving from factories to the service sector. In the future, AI machines could be working alongside humans in many professions and industries such as manufacturing, warehousing, medicine, aviation, law, military defense, and space exploration. Many of them could even replace humans. But could these machines have consciousness similar to that of humans?

Alan Turing who pioneered the thinking computer, designed the Turing test as a benchmark to measure artificial intelligence. A panel of judges having a conversation over a computer network with either another person or a computer program, if at least 30% of them were tricked into thinking that a computer program was a real person, after a five-minute conversation, then it would be considered 'intelligent'. This was successfully achieved in 2014 by a computer program 'Eugene' masquerading as a 13-year-old boy.

Being intelligent is different from being conscious. The Turing Test may not measure sentience.

In science fiction, AI thinks and feels like a human being. But, AI cannot substitute humans in their creativity, imagination, common sense, consciousness, emotional responses, and judgment. In short, machines do not have life.

Here's science fiction vs. reality (as mentioned in the "How

It WorksAnnual 2017 (Vol. 8)".

Possible situations:

- Blade Runner: synthetic humans ('replicants') battling with their creators.
- Westworld: visitors interact with synthetic humanoid hosts that gain consciousness by unlocking their memories.
- Ex Machina: A humanoid AI is created by a programmer who drives her into a murderous act.

Unlikely situations:

- I, Robot: Intelligent humanoids are everywhere. They reveal that they have souls.
- 2001: A Space Odyssey: Sentient artificial life is achieved, and it battles to usurp humanity.
- Terminator: Terminators or cyborgs or AI machines considering humanity as a threat and trying to destroy humanity:

Robotic materials

Household robots and robotic toys are usually made of plastic. New materials are now being tried out to help robots to be flexible, to bend, squeeze, and stretch. "Smart body' uses programmable material such as shape memory polymers and alloys. They can change their shape when exposed to external stimuli such as light or heat. A Shape Memory Alloy (SMA) wire can coil up like a spring when placed in a cup of hot water. Shrinkable plastic (Shrinky Dinks) can be used as self-folding sheets of plastic that could transform into boxes or other 3D shapes automatically. Shape Memory Polymers and Alloys can be used to create artificial muscles.

SMA wire made of Nitinol —a blend of nickel and titanium —can be used as an actuator on very small and flexible robotic bodies. Nitinol is extremely flexible and strong and has been used in orthopedic and cardiac surgery. Its shape memory results from rearrangement of atoms in the Nitinol molecule into different crystalline shapes at different temperatures. Robot builders often use Flexinol, a Nitinol wire made by Dynalloy. It shrinks when heated by an electric current. When cooled, it stretches back to its original shape.

Paper and rubber are also being tried out for transformable robotic bodies because of their advantage in creating various shapes as needed. Origami engineering is used for this purpose.

Developments in material science are also helping robotics to construct robots from new materials such as silicone, spider silk, electroactive polymers that change a robot's size when stimulated by an electric filed, and Ferro fluids.

Biodegradable robots can also be developed now from materials such as PLA (Polylactic Acid), a biodegradable thermoplastic aliphatic polyester that can be made from renewable sources such as cornstarch, tapioca, sugarcane, or other plant material.

An interesting area of research at MIT, Stuttgart University and elsewhere, is programmable matter or creating materials that can morph into any shape. Researchers are trying to create origami robots from programmable matter or creating universal robots such as the T-1000 from the Terminator. With such technologies, we can visualize a world where we can live in reconfigurable houses with efficient usage of space in cities.

Nanorobots

Nanorobots are tiny autonomous machines measuring to the scale of nanometers (smaller than a grain of sand). These can be used to diagnose and treat diseases at the cellular level.

Doctor Robot

In 2013, according to Alec Ross, 1300 surgical robots were sold for an average cost of $1.5 million each. More than 1 million Americans have undergone robotic surgery. The Da Vinci surgical system from Intuitive Surgical in the US can be used for complex surgeries such as cardiac valve repair. The robot translates a surgeon's hand movements into micro movements by the tiny instruments controlled by the robot. Johnson & Johnson has developed the SEDASYS system to automate sedation of patients, to supplement services of anesthesiologists.

Surgical robots can be used in cancer treatment to release radiation at the cellular level or in places where the surgeon's hand cannot reach.

Ukrainian engineering students have developed *Enable Talk*, using flex sensors in the fingers to recognize sign language and then translating it to text on a smartphone via Bluetooth technology. The text is then converted to speech, allowing the deaf and mute to speak.

Space Robots

Mars today is entirely inhabited by robotic rovers. Spirit and Opportunity were sent to the red planet by NASA in 2003. Mars Science Laboratory Rover Curiosity is searching for evidence of life on Mars and it cost $2.6 billion to build. These rovers are six-wheeled, solar-powered robots. They are made autonomous, having to think for themselves which rock to drill into, without waiting for commands from the International Space Station or from the Mission Control Center on the earth. This is because it takes almost 48 minutes to send images to NASA and to get back orders.

Artificial intelligence empowers these rovers to collect and analyze scientific data, and to make decisions without human input. The Autonomous Exploration for Gathering Increased Science (AEGIS) is an autonomous system that was tested an deployed by NASA in May 2016 for Curiosity rover on Martian surface. AEGIS picks out interesting-looking rocks and instructs Curiosity's ChemCam to shoot its lasers at the rocks, to vaporize them, and then analyze their composition. The rover takes its own decision as to what to target for analysis. AEGIS has been taught how to analyze bedrock and to get clues whether Mars had or can support life.

Intelligent systems are giving rise to a new era in space exploration. Satellites orbiting the earth can analyze images that they collect using intelligent systems to detect weather changes, unusual events such as fires, erupting volcano, floods, and to take preventive action in a timely manner.

In the future, intelligent robotic explorers will be sent to explore *Europa* (a moon orbiting Jupiter) or *Alpha Centauri*, our nearest star system, where an earth-like planet has been discovered about 4.4 light-years away.

Brain Computing – Controlling Machines by Thought

Can machines decode human thought? Can we develop technology to help the blind see and the deaf hear? Can human thoughts emanating from the human brain control a robotic arm? Can we communicate with the computer only using our thoughts and brain instead of using the keyboard or mouse or even voice?

Brain machine interfaces are making this a reality. The World Cup 2014 in Brazil was kicked off by an exoskeleton that was powered by brain-machine interfacing and brain computing. Miguel Nicolelis from Duke University developed a mind-controlled exoskeleton. Juliano Pinto, who was paralyzed from chest down used the brain machine interface to pick up Pinto's brainwaves to actuate the exoskeleton and help Juliano to stand and kick the official ball at the games. Improvements in the technology combined with VR (virtual reality) would enable those with spinal-cord injuries to regain movement and feeling in their limbs. Robotic exoskeletons will use hydraulics in the place of muscles, and hinges in the place of joints, to help paralyzed patients to use their limbs. The electrode sensors implanted into the brain will help bearers to control the bionic limbs just by thought.

The Economist of January 4, 2018, in the article titled *'Using Thought to Control Machines'* stated that Brain-

Computer Interfaces may change what it means to be human.

Miguel Nicolelis, a systems neurophysiologist of Duke University, in his book *'Beyond Boundaries: The New Neuroscience of Connecting Brains with Machines And How It Will Change Our lives'* (2011), explains how sensors can pick up the signals or brain storms created by the neural circuits created by the hundreds of billions of cells in the human brain. These signals can then be directed to actuate a desired physical action.

Brain Computer Interfaces (BCI) have been a subject of research since the 1990s. Electrodes implanted in the brain can capture electrical signals from the brain that can be digitized and interpreted by computer software to act on those signals, as in activating a prosthetic arm. Today BCI technology enables a paralyzed man to feed himself using his own paralyzed hand. Implants in his brain detect neural signals from his motor cortex that are generated by his thoughts to move his arms. These signals are processed into commands to activate the electrodes implanted in the arms to stimulate the muscles.

Brain computing will be particularly useful for people with disabilities, for veterans who have lost their limbs, those who have been paralyzed from stroke, and for old people on wheel chairs. Vehicle drivers, aircraft pilots and those controlling robots on the shop-floor in factories or in inaccessible areas as in a battlefield, can use this computing power effectively. Remote control of machines is also possible.

Computer games controlled by the brain would be an

exciting application area.

The story of Saqib Shaikh, Software Engineer of Microsoft, is a case in point. Saqib lost his eyesight at the age of seven. As a Microsoft Developer he developed an app, the intelligent software system called Seeing AI, to help the blind or visually impaired see with AI. Using the application, the blind can read out text from posters or menus by clicking a photo. The application guides them to take the photo. Smart sunglass wearable can help the blind take a picture and interpret the surroundings through an audio feedback system.

Cochlear implants help the deaf to hear by converting sound into electrical signals to be decoded by the brain.

Elon Musk's company Neuralink is engaged in developing brain-computer interfaces.

Facebook also has been involved with developing brain-computer technologies. Facebook is developing the technology to convert thought to text-typing.

Braintree (founded by Bryan Johnson) is focusing on neuro-prosthesis by programming the neural code of the human brain. Neuro-prosthetics involves stimulating the nervous system to restore the lost function of sensation or movement. It combines principles of neuro science and bio-medical engineering.

Cognitive Computing & Neuro Science

We may be on the threshold of developing a human being with a fully artificial human brain.

LIVING WITH INTELLIGENT MACHINES

Today disabled persons can control their prosthetic limbs using their implanted brain components. Deep-brain stimulation via electrodes is helping people to control Parkinson's disease.

In the future, people may be able to communicate telepathically with each other and with machines.

The challenges are in developing brain implants that can interact directly with the neurons. Consider the enormity of the task when we are dealing with 85 billion neurons in the human brain. Existing implants involve wires that pass through the skull, communicating with a few hundred of the billions of neurons. The human brain is still an unexplored territory. Reportedly, brain computing may be next digital frontier.

Chapter 6

HARNESSING THE POWER OF BIG DATA

"Where is the wisdom we have lost in knowledge? Where is the knowledge we have lost in information?"

-TS Eliot – 'Choruses from the Rock'

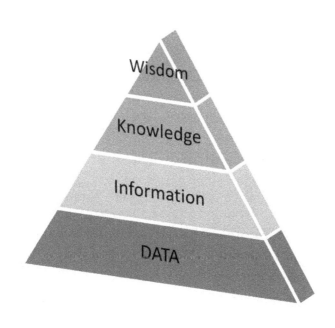

Walmart (the world's largest retailer with over 2 million employees and 20,000 stores in 28 countries) is using a private data cloud to process 2.5 petabytes of information every hour to analyze sales of millions of products to millions of people. This helps in having the right products in the right places at the right time. It helps in supply chain management, product pricing, and customer service. Walmart established Data Cafe --a state-of-the-art big data analytics hub at their Bentonville, Arkansas headquarters. Walmart uses Hadoop, the distributed data storage and data management system for their big data analytics. Other technologies used include Spark, Cassandra, R and SAS for developing analytical applications.

Big Data Analytics is helping Walmart to compete with Amazon and Alibaba in the retail business space.

Data as Knowledge Source

Data that is the source of knowledge, is becoming the main resource and coin of the emerging digital economy and information society. But data will be second only to intellectual capital that will be required to extract intelligence and knowledge from data.

With the growth and use of computers and smart phones there is an explosion in the growth of data and information. With the widespread adoption of connected devices and Internet of Things (IoT), massive volume of sensor data is to be managed. The rapidly increasing volume of data, in structured and unstructured forms in the form of emails, presentations, video, photos, images, audio, and in multi-language formats, is providing great challenges and opportunities.

Analyzing all forms of data can lead to vital information and intelligence. Data becomes a critical corporate asset. Harnessing its power can provide value, help to solve complex problems, and provide competitive advantage to corporations that can act promptly on data to create products and services needed by the customers.

As described by Davenport and Harris (2017) in their book *'Competing on Data Analytics'*, data analytics involves creating insights from data, going beyond bar charts and regression analysis to enable organizations develop successful business strategies. Data Science and analytics are rewriting the rules of competition, creating business strategies based on data analysis covering the entire gamut of business-- Marketing, Supply Chain, Finance, M&A, HR, Operations, and R&D.

From Business Intelligence to Data Analytics

Business Intelligence

Traditionally businesses have captured their data in relational database systems (RDBMS), leading to creation of data marts for various business segments and consolidated them at the enterprise level into data warehouses. Various online analytical processing tools (OLAP) techniques are used to query the data and to generate enterprise-wide reports or dashboards.

While data marts and data warehouses are created from 'structured data' in legacy database systems, consolidated unstructured data is now referred to as 'data lakes'. Data warehouses, data marts, and data lakes now co-exist in organizations.

Evolution of Data Analytics

Davenport and Harris detail the evolution of data analytics from earlier stages. **Analytics 1.0** was focused on descriptive analytics (Business Intelligence) or what happened in the past. Today the best companies focus on predictive analytics focused on the future and prescriptive analytics on changes required for optimizing operations. In the earlier stages, data marts and data warehouses were created from transactional data to aid in data analysis and business intelligence, mostly for decision support. The challenges were in validating the data, in use of ETL (Extract, Transform and Load) tools, in structuring the data to conform to RDBMS systems, in building and maintaining the data marts and organizational data warehouses.

Challenges of big data

Data analysis has shifted from analyzing transactional data to data on products and services. Machine learning and AI technologies have helped in automating the analytics process.

Analytics 2.0 started sometime in 2006 or so when Google, eBay, PayPal, LinkedIn, Yahoo, and others had to deal with unstructured and voluminous data. Doug Cutting and Mike Cafarella developed Hadoop, for storing large amounts of data across distributed servers, for parallel processing.

Hadoop was focused on data storage. Pig, Hive, Python, R, were developed and used for processing big data in batch mode. Spark evolved to process streaming data in real-time.

Practitioners of big data analytics called themselves data scientists. New computing architectures such as cloud computing posed further challenges.

Analytical competition

The focus on analytical competition and building analytical capability became a need with **Analytics 3.0** when data analytics had to be integrated with production processes and systems, and supply chain management. The focus was on operational analytics.

Some operational analytics cases can be cited. UPS started the ORION project for driver routing saving UPS half a billion dollars in labor and fuel costs. GE had to analyze sensor data from jet engines, gas turbines, windmills, MRI machines, etc. Monsanto in their Climate Pro analytics application uses weather, crop and soil data to suggest optimal times for farmers to plant, water, and harvest their crop.

Analytics 4.0 (autonomous analytics) was further developed with the aid of artificial intelligence and cognitive technologies such as machine learning and deep learning. Deep learning, based on artificial neural networks (with multiple layers of features or variables to predict) requires large amounts of data to learn on, and high level of computing power to solve complex problems

Data Analytics can be a source of business innovation leading to strategic business advantage, as pointed out by Sam Ransbotham and David Kiron in '*Analytics as a Source of Business Innovation*' (*MIT Sloan Management Review, February 28, 2017*). The companies that were surveyed indicated that data governance led to innovation and business strategy changes and competitive advantage. Companies that are noted for data-driven innovation are General Electric, Google, IBM, Airbnb, and Uber. Bridgestone and Nedbank Group Ltd. are also cited as an example of traditional companies using data analytics to improve their existing operations and to create new business.

Big Data

The astronomical data collected by Sloan Digital Sky Survey that started in 2000 using the telescope in New Mexico had around 140 Terabytes of data, and this exceeded the data collected throughout the entire history of astronomy. Similarly, when scientists decoded the human genome in 2003, it took them almost a decade to sequence the three billion base pairs of DNA. Now this can be done in a day. Seven billion shares change hands every day in US equity markets. Google processes more than 24 petabytes of data every day. Facebook gets more than 10 million photos uploaded every hour. Twitter has 400 million tweets a day.

Big Data is continuously generated by humans, machines, and sensors. Typical sources are: enterprise data, public data, transactional data, social media data, sensor data from Internet of Things (IoT) devices, and location information from GPS.

How do we deal with such massive volume of data in structured or unstructured formats?

Big Data involves

- large volume of data (petabytes)
- high velocity (real-time)
- wide variety (text, video, images, audio, web content, structured and unstructured data).

Some sources of big data are sensors, smartphones, tablets, and social media.

Sensor data could be RFID tags, data from smart meters, medical devices, or GPS data. RFID data is used for supply chain management and inventory control, and in tracking containers from origin to destination.

Unstructured data

Some examples of unstructured data are:

- Satellite images (weather data, Google Earth images)
- Scientific data (seismic imagery, atmospheric data, high energy physics)
- Photographs and video
- Radar or sonar data
- Text within documents and emails
- Social media data

- Mobile data (text messages, location information)
- Website content

MapReduce, Hadoop & Spark

Earlier, supercomputing technology was required to process high volumes of data. Collating and analyzing such data in real time became a challenge. MapReduce, Hadoop, and Big Table were technological innovations in this area.

Google developed the Map Reduce and Google File System to deal with analysis of massive data by splitting the data into chunks, processing them independently and then combining the results. This was done in a batch processing mode. Big Table was also developed by Google as a distributed storage system to manage highly scalable structured data.

Doug Cutting, a software consultant now at Cloudera, developed the Hadoop system in 2006 to sift through massive datasets quickly and in a cost-effective way. He mimicked Google's map-reduce system that analyzes big complex data by splitting the data into smaller chunks and then collating the results.

The Hadoop system that he created was named after his son's toy elephant. Yahoo!, Facebook, Walt Disney, the New York Times, Samsung are some of the companies that use Hadoop for analyzing their massive amounts of unstructured data.

Hadoop is an Apache-managed software framework derived from MapReduce and Big Table, allowing MapReduce applications to run on large hardware clusters, supporting massively scalable distributed file system supporting petabytes of data, and massively scalable MapReduce engine computing the results in batch mode processing.

Hadoop includes the HDFS (for data storage), MapReduce (for bulk data processing), Spark (for real-time data processing), and YARN (for resource management and scheduling). A Hadoop cluster could consist of thousands of nodes.

MapReduce is implemented in Java. Spark's native language is Scala. Python can be used to program Spark jobs (using PySpark library). SQL can be used to query data from the HDFS using tools like Hive and SparkSQL.

Traditional RDBMS cannot handle big data demands. NoSQL databases that are non-relational, distributed database systems, were developed to meet big data demands to query graph databases, document databases (MongoDB), key-values stores (Apache Cassandra & HBase), and column family stores. NoSQL applications Apache Cassandra and MongoDB are used for data storage and real-time processing. MongoDB is suitable for document storage and retrieval.

Data Science

Data Science has evolved from Business Intelligence to focus more on predictive analytics.

Big Data Analytics

Finding patterns in data is the most challenging aspect of

data analysis. In their book *'Big Data'*, Viktor Mayer-Schonberger and Kenneth Cukier describe how 'big data' can be used by powerful algorithms to identify hidden relationships between seemingly unrelated things. NSA uses data analytics to fight terrorism, and online retailers predict customer buying patterns.

Data Analytics today involves massive unstructured data. Traditional relational database systems or even file systems used by mainframes are not suitable to handle such data. HADOOP, HDFS (Hadoop Distributed Data File Systems), MapReduce, and SPARK evolved to process such data. With quantum computing technologies appearing on the horizon, massive computing power will be in the hands of business leaders and technologists to analyze massive data, and to extract relevant information for informed decision making and strategy development.

Data analytics can transform organizations and the economy. Data analytics capabilities in integrated into operations and strategies, can transform organizations. Wal-Mart Stores uses data analytics to adjust its inventory levels and prices. FedEx determines delivery routes. Airlines and telecommunications companies identify their best customers.

Data Analytics is more focused on knowledge discovery, in uncovering unknown facts or insights into massive amounts of data—structured, unstructured, semi-structured, streaming, etc.

Analytics Software

Some of the Analytical Software currently used can be listed here:

- Excel
- Statistical Software: Minitab or Stata
- Data Visualization and descriptive analytics: Qlik, Tableau, MicroStrategy, Oracle Hyperion, IBM Cognos
- Descriptive, Predictive, and Prescriptive analytics software (SAS, SPSS/ IBM)
- Prediction Industry applications: FICO
- Reporting & Analytical Modules of Enterprise Systems (SAP Business Objects, Oracle)
- Statistical Programming Open-Source (R, Python)

Big Data Injection Tools for IoT Sensor Data - Microsoft

Microsoft Azure cloud computing infrastructure provides facility to capture IoT sensor information using its IoT hubs and Azure gateway services, to perform stream processing using *Azure HDInsight*, to provide real-time dashboards and storage.

Some of the tools used are listed below:

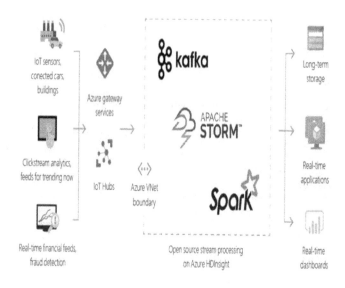

Fig. Courtesy: Microsoft

Apache Squoop is a data transference tool to transfer data between a relational system and the Hadoop Distributed File System (HDFS), using clusters of servers to store the data. HDFS distributes storage tasks across these clusters.

Apache Kafka: is a distributed messaging system acting as a message broker, pushing and pulling message into and from HDFS.

Apache Flume is a distributed system to handle log and event data, to transfer massive quantities of unstructured data to and from the HDFS.

Data Analytics using Amazon Web Services (AWS)

Amazon is providing global cloud computing services known as Amazon Web Services (AWS) since 2006. AWS serves over 1 million customers in over 190 countries, providing highly available infrastructure platform in multiple locations worldwide divided into regions and availability zones.

Amazon Elastic Compute Cloud (EC2) is a web service providing resizable compute capacity in the Amazon cloud. *Amazon Virtual Private Cloud (Amazon VPC)* allows you provision a logically separated section of AWS cloud to launch your AWS resources in a virtual network. Using VPN connectivity, the corporate network can be extended to the Amazon VPC. *AWS Direct* Connect also provides dedicated circuit connectivity.

You can obtain and configure virtual servers in Amazon's data centers, using various operating systems and configurations of memory, CPU, storage, etc. For back-end web developers *AWS Lambda* can be used for running your back-end code on AWS compute fleet of Amazon EC2 instances.

AWS Elastic Beanstalk enables fast deployment of web applications on AWS. Developers upload their application code, and the service handles resource provisioning, load balancing, auto scaling, and monitoring. It supports a variety of web platforms such as PHP, Java, Python, Ruby, Node.js, .NET, and GO.

Amazon Storage Services and Infrastructure

Amazon's Simple Storage Service (Amazon S3) provides cost-effective object storage (HTML pages, source code files, image files, and encrypted data) that can be accessed using HTTP-based protocols. *Amazon Elastic Block Store (EBS)* provides persistent block-level storage volumes for use with EC2 instances.

Amazon Glazier is a low-cost service for data archiving and data-backup.

Amazon CloudFront is a content delivery web service enabling global transfer of dynamic, static, or streaming, or interactive content to end-users around the globe.

Database Services are provided by SQL and non-SQL database services. *Amazon RDS* (Relational Database Service) is a relational database. Amazon *DynamoDB* is a noSQL database service supporting both document and key/value data models. *Amazon Redshift* is a peta-byte scale data warehouse service.

Analytics services: *Amazon Kinesis* is a streaming data platform for loading, storing and analyzing streaming data. The stream data can store the data in S3, ElasticSearch, DynamoDB or RedShift.

For batch jobs involving traditional ETL (extract transform, and load) processes for BI Analytics, *Amazon Data Pipeline* is more suitable than Amazon Kinesis.

Amazon EMR (Elastic Map Reduce) provides a fully managed, on demand Hadoop framework that includes Apache Hadoop, MapR Hadoop, and additional tools and applications such as Hive, Pig, Spark, or Presto.

Predictive Analytics & Data Mining

Data mining is used to find patterns in data using

algorithms such as decision tree, artificial neural networks, logistic regression, and clustering methods. These algorithms are explained in detail in the next chapter on algorithms.

Insight into Data

Many business problems can be described as classification problems. Is this a fraudulent or legitimate insurance claim? Can this customer be trusted? What is the probability that this cancer patient will survive for 5 years?

In all these situations, decisions must be data-driven and predictive analytics can help in better and informed decision-making. It helps in identifying patterns and relationships in data to provide actionable insights into the organization.

Various data mining techniques can be used for this purpose. Statistical analysis is fairly well known. Statistical parameters such as mean, median, mode, statistical distribution, correlation and regression techniques and visual graphics help to make data meaningful.

But today machine learning techniques are gaining ground. Data mining and classification techniques include supervised and unsupervised learning techniques.

Machine Learning & Machine Intelligence

"The volume of data continues to double every three years as information pours in from digital platforms, wireless sensors, virtual-reality applications, and billions of mobile phones. Data-storage capacity has increased, while its cost has plummeted. Data scientists now have unprecedented computing power at their disposal, and they are devising algorithms that are ever more sophisticated."

Machine Learning, deep learning and supervised learning algorithms can help find patterns in data and produce knowledge and intelligence on a scale that was not found imaginable so far.

Content and Text Analytics

Document content contains unstructured data. Metadata about documents can assist in grouping and classifying them for various types of access control. Some other use cases are:

- Document summary or abstract, specifying the key concepts, key terms, important features, and one or two-line summary of the contents
- Sentiments, opinions or emotions expressed
- Grade scores
- Category of content, news (can help recommender systems to link it with users)
- Linked documents and information retrieval

Some of the Analytical Tools used are:

- R Programming Language
- Apache Mahout (free implementation of machine learning algorithms for data mining and Hadoop clusters)
- Bayesian Networks
- Bayesian Networks represent probability distributions of attributes as a network of nodes

(attributes) using a directed acyclic graph (DAG). Bayesian networks are found to be better for conditional probability distribution than other methods such as Naïve Bayes, Logistic Regression or Decision Trees.

- Rapid Miner is a useful tool for data mining using machine learning algorithms

Why predictions fail?

Thomas Bayes, an English minister of the 18th century, is credited with the Bayes Theorem that has influenced predictions based on probabilities. The posterior probability (probability that a future event may happen) is based on three conditional prior probabilities.

Accuracy of the predictive probability using Bayes theorem depends on the assumptions made. As pointed out by Nate Silver in *'The signal and the Noise—Why So Many Predictions Fail – But Some Don't'* (2012), the a-priori probabilities can be contaminated by bias and subjectivity. How objective is the data sampling that calculates the prior probabilities, as in political poll results prediction? The nature of the sample population, the randomness of the sampling, the volume of the dataset, and validity and reliability of data, are important considerations for reducing errors in estimation.

Nate Silver also points out that data is useless without context.

Data-driven decision making

Machine Learning and Deep Learning can be used

effectively for analyzing voluminous data in data analytics and pattern recognition to support decision making. IBM Watson is today employed in cancer detection and research by UT MD Anderson Cancer Center in Houston TX, USA. The same technology is used by Wall Street firms to analyze massive amounts of financial and investment data, and to advise on investments and investment market trends. Data Analytics can be effectively used in analysis of financial transactions to detect fraud and can also be used for security event data analysis.

Data Management & Storage

New database systems and data storage systems are evolving to provide more efficient capture, storage and retrieval of data. Traditional file systems were replaced by relational database management systems. Today non-SQL databases are emerging to deal with big data and unstructured data.

Virtual storage systems like NAS and SAN systems have made storage and retrieval more cost-effective. Redundant data centers or Disaster Recovery Centers help to create backups and to restore data in the case of a disaster.

Data Availability

The focus of data governance also must include data availability when required. Availability of the networks, systems, and applications that process the data, must be given adequate attention. Business Continuity Plans and Disaster Recovery plans, data classification, criticality and sensitivity and business impact analysis, are part of this process to ensure availability of mission critical data.

Integrating siloed information systems and databases within an enterprise would be a major challenge for data engineers.

Trusting data

Can we trust the data we analyze? Integrity of data and validation processes become important criteria before data is analyzed. In his article, *'In Data We Trust'*, Jeff Wilson, Chief Marketing Officer of Profisee, describes the problem of trustworthiness of data.

It is here that 'data governance' becomes crucial. Master Data Management (MDM) technology is considered by corporations as the solution to enterprise data governance for providing reliable data.

The challenge here arises because data may be dispersed within an organization in multiple systems and multiple locations. Consolidating all the data, cleansing the data and feeding it for analysis and for generating actionable intelligence, is a major challenge. Consider the data that is required for sales and marketing, to target marketing segments and to determine which products and services to focus on.

Security Requirements of Big Data

When considering Big Data, security and privacy aspects of the data must be considered. These include:

- Data Access
- Application Access
- Data encryption

- Risk assessment
- Threat detection

Application Programming Interfaces (APIs) and data feeds from various data sources are important factors for successful big data implementation. The physical infrastructure has to consider a geographically distributed data system controlled by distributed networks and databases. A distributed file system has to be taken into account, in addition to security of distributed networks, communication systems, applications and databases including NoSQL databases. Identity and access management systems would be an integral part of the security infrastructure.

Data Confidentiality & Privacy

Data Governance and Security must also include protection of privacy and confidentiality of data. Many privacy regulations are in force to protect customer privacy, confidentiality of financial information in storage and in transit. European Union has come forward with its GDPR (General Data Protection Regulations) that would come into force from May 2018.

Appropriate data classification mechanisms, protective mechanisms such as encryption, role-based access control, identity and access management solutions, are all part of the data protection mechanisms that would be required to be implemented in organizations.

The barriers

Some of the barriers that may prevent an effective data

analytics program are:

- Lack of analytical talent
- System silos, data silos, data ownership issues, and integration of data across various sources.
- Issues of Interoperability and data sharing
- Dealing with unstructured data
- Data access issues
- Leadership skepticism
- Data quality

All these point to the need for effective data governance function and processes in organizations. Data and analytics must be integrated into every part of the organization. Organizations must have a data strategy.

Big Data in Practice

Bernard Marr in the book *'Big Data in Practice'* (2016) explains 'how 45 successful companies used big data analytics to deliver extraordinary results'. According to him big data is a game-changer and the companies listed are using big data to create strategic value.

Amazon uses predictive analytics to get a 360-degree view of customers. Amazon is not just an online bookshop any more. It is one of the world's largest retailer of physical goods (stored in its fulfillment centers), virtual goods such as e-books and streaming video. Amazon Web Services provide cloud computing services. Amazon is also a producer of goods and services, commissioning films and TV shows, building and marketing electronic goods such as tablets, TVs, and streaming hardware. With the acquisition of Whole Foods, it is also into food supermarket business.

'Everything under one roof' supermarket model confuses the customer. Amazon uses the recommendation engine based on big data analytics capturing information on customer behavior of its 250 million customers. Amazon also has around 2 million third-party Amazon Marketplace sellers.

Big Data is at the center of the business of Google, Facebook, Apple, and Microsoft -- the technology giants.

Facebook, the world's largest social network, uses big data to capture information on its 1.5 billion customers, who use it free to read news, create their personal content, and to make buying decisions based on advertisements and customer recommendations.

Facebook attracted two million active advertisers in 2016. They pay Facebook for their ads. Data collected about users browsing Facebook is used to target them with advertisements. Facebook created the HipHop for MySQL compiler for more efficient CPU operations. It uses its own distributed storage system based on Hadoop's **HBase** to manage storage. It uses Apache's Hive for real-time analytics of user data.

Google: Google's indexing system indexes the entire Internet content used by Google Search and requires around 100 petabytes (100 million gigabytes) of storage. Google PageRank algorithm searches and filters the content to list the top ones based on the keywords of a specific search. Google has the world's biggest online advertising network using big data technology.

Apple with its leadership in the mobile phone (iPhone) and iPad market has information about the millions of its customers. Apple Watch, launched in 2015, has sensors such as heart rate monitor to track user's activities and health. It shares this data with IBM's Watson Health cloud-based healthcare analytics. Apple's Siri voice recognition systems capture voice data and upload it to cloud analytics platforms for analyzing speech patterns. In March 2015, Apple acquired Foundation DB, a database used for big data applications. Apple Music Service with its acquisition of Beats Music is trying to capture the streaming music market dominated by Pandora, Spotify, and Google Music. Apple uses Teradata equipment to store the massive data generated by Apple users.

Microsoft's big data analytics cloud-based platform combines SQL SERVER database system with their HDInsight Hadoop distribution. Microsoft is also offering Microsoft Azure cloud-based systems focusing on machine-to-machine data analytics targeted at IoT devices. Toyota uses Microsoft HD Insight on Microsoft Azure cloud computing platform for real-time processing of sensor information from millions of Toyota cars being manufactured globally.

IBM Watson is the best example of the combination of big data analytics using IBM Watson's deep learning and cognitive computing technology.

The Bosch Group, a 170-year old company based in Germany, uses data analytics for intelligent fleet management, vehicle-charging infrastructures, energy management, security video analysis, and so on. The company created a Software Innovations Group focusing heavily on big data, analytics, and the 'Internet of Things'.

General Electric's manufacturing divisions use big data analytics to analyze streaming sensor data from turbines, locomotives, jet engines, and medical imaging devices. GE has developed 'Predix', a platform for building 'industrial internet' applications.

Schneider Electric

Schneider of France, existing for 170 years, originally focused on iron, steel, and armaments. Schneider today focuses on energy optimization, building automation, and utility management. Its Advanced Distribution Management System monitors and controls network devices and manages service outages. Using big data analytics, it integrates millions of data points on network performance for utility companies.

The Dark Side of Big Data

Cathy O'Neil's book *'Weapons of Math Destruction'* (2017) points to the dangers of big data analytics and the algorithms that drive it. The author points out that big data is as good as the people who create the algorithms that process the data for various uses. These affect the common man in getting loans, making health insurance payments, getting a job, etc. Just as these mathematical models created by the algorithms are powerful, there are risks and a dark side to the process. A model's blind spots reflecting the judgments and biases of its creators, may lead to wrong results and actions. They can create inequality and threaten democracy.

The book is an eye-opener and pointer to the need to be careful in using Big Data solutions. The author cautions us against using the analytical results blindly without examining the underlying assumptions and the validity of the data.

Wisdom lies in Small Data

Martin Lindstrom's book '*Small Data-The Tiny Clues That Uncover Huge Trends*' (2016) New York: Picador) is insightful. Lindstrom, as a marketer and brand-building expert, reminds us not to lose sight of the consumer's psychology and mind, while trying to get insight into big data. He tells us that the needle is rarely found in the big data haystack. The experience of Capital One would vouch for this. Too much reliance on marketing analytics and big data had ignored Capital One's brand. (Peter Horst and Robert Duboff, '*Don't Let Big Data Bury Your Brand*', HBR, November 2015). Probably wisdom lies in small data.

Chapter 7

IN CODE WE TRUST --THE ALGORITHMIC WORLD

At the heart of emerging technologies is the software code encapsulating the algorithms and processing logic of the computer applications. Programmers, who are better

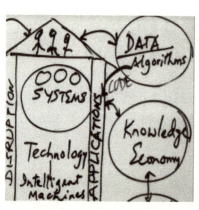

known as software development engineers and systems analysts and architects, develop the software applications. These applications power the complex systems driving the disruptive technologies. Various programming languages are used for developing these applications for various operating systems and processors. In the place of COBOL and FORTRAN, C or machine languages used in legacy systems, today we have .NET, C#, JAVA, Python, Scala, R, JavaScript, PHP, Ruby on Rails, etc. as programming or scripting languages.

The computer programs convert into software code the algorithms capturing the logic and data flow. All system problems are analyzed, and the solutions are captured by the algorithms that are designed to solve systems problems.

Algorithms capture human intelligence. They create the knowledge to drive machines and human systems. Algorithms give power to data analytics, helping to create insight into big data, converting data into information and knowledge.

The powerful combination of human intelligence and creativity leading to innovative products and services, will create 'the mathematical corporations' of the future, as pointed out by Sullivan & Zutavern (2017) in their book 'The Mathematical Corporation – Where Machine Intelligence + Human Ingenuity Achieve the Impossible'. In mathematical corporations, data-driven decision making will be the norm. Data and algorithms will drive these successful corporations.

MACHINE LEARNING

Artificial intelligence is often associated with machine learning or the algorithms that drive artificial intelligence applications including robotics. Machine learning enables computers to learn from past data. Since the 1990s the 'spam filter' powered by machine learning algorithms have been part of email systems.

Machine learning algorithms are the lifeblood of organizations such as Google or Facebook. At Amazon, machine learning algorithms are used for demand forecasting, product search ranking, product recommendations, replacements, fraud detection, translations, etc.

Deep learning algorithms (also known as Artificial Neural Networks or ANN) can be used for early disease detection, for increasing crop yields, natural language processing, and speech analysis. Deep learning makes facial recognition, image processing, speech and voice recognition, and language translation much easier. Thanks to deep learning algorithms, today we have Siri, Cortana, and Alexa, the digital virtual assistants that are activated by voice control. Deep learning also drives many computer games. In 2016 researchers at the Icahn School of Medicine at Mount Sinai, New York, used deep learning to analyze 75,000 patient records against 78 diseases. They were able to predict severe diabetes, schizophrenia, and various cancers with high predictive accuracy. Autonomous vehicles use deep learning to interpret sensor data and to recognize hazards on the road. In 2016, a Tesla autonomous car drove into the back of a stalled van. It is too early to place too much reliance on the algorithms when safety is involved.

Deep learning essentially uses artificial neural network techniques and reinforcement learning.

Machine Learning Algorithms

Machine learning algorithms can be broadly classified into supervised and unsupervised learning algorithms.

Unsupervised Learning techniques - Clustering

Data Clustering helps in finding structures within a dataset when the structure is not obvious. The clustering algorithms can create subgroups within the unlabeled dataset by extracting groupings or categories with similarities.

K-Means Clustering Algorithm and Nearest Neighbor algorithm are among the algorithms commonly used for data clustering.

Clustering can be used for market or customer segmentation based on geography or size, finding related news articles, tweets, blogs, image recognition, etc.

Supervised Learning

Data Classification techniques, in contrast to data clustering, rely on prior labeling the data as belonging to a group. Based on labeled data, the classification algorithm predicts the classification of unlabeled data.

Data Classification involves first the learning stage when training data is run through the classifier algorithm to teach the model the relationships and classification rules from the historical (training) data.

In the second stage or prediction stage, the model can predict the new class labels for the new test data.

The algorithms used are:

- Decision Trees
- Naïve Bayes

171

- Neural Networks
- Markov Model (used in systems following a chain of linked events, where what happens next depends only on the current state of the system).
- Support Vector Machines

Support Vector Machines

(SVMs) are suitable for data problems that cannot easily be solved by algorithms such as K-Nearest neighbors, Logistic Regression, or Decision Trees for non-linear data regression as well as for classification problems.

They can be used for

- Binary and multi-class classification and regression analysis, but it is mostly used as a binary classifier because of enhanced processing requirements.
- Handles overfitting, noisy data, and outliers
- Can handle situations with many variables
- Automatic detection of non-linear data using kernel functions.

SVMs find application in many image-recognition problems particularly in medical diagnosis. The algorithm is also useful for textual classification as in Natural Language Processing. However, it has limited applicability in analysis of big data.

Random Forests

To improve the performance of decision trees, an ensemble or forest of trees is built using random sampling and bagging methods. A random forest of trees created will use a voting method to identify the optimal solution.

Applications of Machine Learning methods

Some of the applications of machine learning methods are listed below:

- Linear regression (predictions of sales forecasts, prizing optimization, marketing optimization, financial risk assessment)
- Logistic regression (to predict customer churn)
- Naive Bayes Classifier: categorize products, customers.
- K- Means clustering: cost modeling and customer segmentation (for marketing optimization)
- Hierarchical clustering: modeling business processes, segment customers
- K-nearest neighbor classification: text-document classification, financial distress prediction modeling, competitor analysis
- Principal component analysis: dimensionality reduction method for detecting fraud, for speech recognition, spam detection.
- Reinforcement learning (or semi-supervised learning) maximizes rewards by adapting decisions.

Reinforcement Learning

Reinforcement Learning was used by Google DeepMind's AlphaGo. The program is instructed on what it must do. As it progresses towards its goal, positive actions are reinforced by a reward scheme. It uses artificial neural network and deep learning algorithms.

Importance of training data and feature selection for predictive accuracy

As pointed out by Aurelien Geron (2017), choosing sufficient training data with enough number of relevant features is important for creating an effective predictive model. Main challenges of machine learning include:

- Insufficient quantity of training data: For complex problems such as image or speech recognition, millions of examples would be required.

- Non-representative training data may result in inaccurate predictions. Very large samples could also be non-representative if the sampling is flawed (called the sampling bias)

- Poor quality training data, with errors, outliers, and noise or training data with missing features

- Irrelevant features: Feature selection, feature extraction and feature reduction using dimensionality reduction algorithms would help. New features could be added by gathering new data.

- Overfitting the training data: The model is too complex but fits the training data well. For new data with fresh attributes, prediction performance degrades. Simplify the model with fewer features or parameters, reduce the number of attributes in the training data; gather more training data; reduce noise in the training data by fixing data errors and by removing outliers. Relevancy of features must be examined.

- Underfitting the training data: The model is too simple to learn the underlying structure of the data.

Add more parameters, feed better features, reduce constraints on the model that restrict the features.

Feature extraction

It is important to identify relevant features of a data set to create a predictive model. Reducing the number of features is necessary to produce an optimal model. Domain experts can help in identifying relevant features. This process also can be automated by using clustering techniques and principal component analysis method.

Features extracted must also be weighted within the model.

The accuracy of a predictive model based on the extracted features can be tested using cross-validation technique. The sample data is split into two parts: a training set with 90% data and a test set with 10% of the data. These two sets can be used to test the predictive accuracy of the model built.

If the environment changes, the predictive model may not be applicable.

Data Mining Algorithms

Decision Tree is a powerful data mining tool. An example is a physician trying to predict breast cancer for a patient based on the patient's attributes. For this he has historical data and experiential knowledge of the relative importance of various factors that contribute to breast cancer.

Some of the variables are:

- clump thickness

175

- uniformity of cell size
- uniformity of cell shape
- marginal adhesion
- single epithelial cell size
- bare nuclei
- bland chromatin
- mitoses

A decision tree can be created for breast cancer diagnosis data.

This would help in identifying factors that are important for classifying a tumor as benign or malignant.

Common decision tree types are:

- CHAID (Chi-Squared Automatic Interaction Detection based on Chi-Square Test of Independence)
- CART (Classification and Regression Tree) using binary recursive partitioning. CART produces binary (two-way) splits.
- C5.0 along with C4.5 and ID3
- QUEST (Quick Unbiased Efficient Statistical Tree) provides for speedy processing when dealing with large amounts of data

These can be used for predictive analysis using both categorical and continuous variables.

KNIME, ORANGE, and other tools/ software can be used to create decision trees.

Neural Networks

Artificial Neural Networks (ANN) is a data mining and predictive modeling technique that mimics the human brain. Neuron is a cell that carries information through the brain and human body using neuro-transmitters or chemicals that transmit electrical signals.

Multi-layer perceptron: Each input is multiplied by its weight and added up to give the output. Such a linear model is not applicable to neural networks that need various intermediate layers (hidden layers) considering the connections between various input neurons.

Radial Basis Function (RBF) is a slight modification of the Multi-Layer Perceptron (MLP). Bayesian Networks are also used in neural network analysis.

The Kohonen Network is a neural network that is used for clustering.

A neural network filters the features at various layers and then gives the output. The layers are hidden, and weights are used to represent the connection between the neurons. It can process only numeric and continuous information. To process continuous variables, they have to be transformed into a series of binary values.

Deep learning is an improvement over neural networks for processing large data sets such as Big Data, and to increase the number of layers for processing. Improvements in CPUs and GPUs (Graphical Processing Units) made deep learning a possibility. Deep learning became useful in situations such as image processing where it was required to learn complex features from several images. In the

IN CODE WE TRUST --THE ALGORITHMIC WORLD

Google Brain Project Andrew Ng and Jeff Dean team used a cluster of around 16,000 computers to perform deep learning computing using YouTube videos using more than 1 billion weights.

Clustering methods

Without relying on historical data for classifying data, data can be classified and separated out into groups using clustering methods, also known as 'unsupervised learning algorithms'. K-Means is a popular clustering method.

Logistical Regression

Linear regression can be used when we are dealing with continuous variables.

Categorical variables with binary outcomes, can be dealt with for classification and predictive modeling using decision trees or neural networks. Logistic regression is the traditional technique using a probabilistic determination of the outcome for an option.

Logistical Regression uses a *logit function* to compute odds (the chance that a given outcome will happen) for each option. The predicted category has the most favorable odds.

Examples:

- loan: Repaid or Not Repaid
- Tumor: benign or malignant
- Preferred drink: water, coffee, coke

Machine Learning Tools

Though R and Python are used for programming normal machine learning tasks, there are several tools that can be used for analytics tasks using machine learning algorithms. Commonly used statistical packages SAS, Stata, and SPSS are used for statistical analysis.

Machine learning frameworks are used to study the particular domain-specific problems before performing programming using machine learning tools. Tools automate many of the programming tasks. Some of the useful machine learning tools are listed below:

- Apache Singa: a deep learning framework for natural language processing and image recognition.
- Apache Spark MLib: is a large library of premade solutions
- Caffe: is used for deep learning involving vision tasks and learning from images. It has the pretrained CaffeNet neural network. It uses C++ for the underlying code but has Python and MATLAB interfaces.
- Google TensorFlow: relies on *data flow graphs* that define deep learning algorithms to process data batches (tensors).
- Oxdata H2O: the prepackaged libraries can directly access Hadoop Distributed File Store (HDFS) using Java, Python, R, and Scala.
- Nervana Neon: uses CPUs, GPUs, or the custom Nervana hardware to perform machine learning tasks. The framework relies mostly on Python and C++ code.

179

- Shogun: the libraries can be used by various languages C++, Java, Python, C#, Ruby, R, Lua, Octave, and Matlab.

- Weka (http://www.cs.waikato.ac.nz/ml/weka) is a collection of machine learning algorithms written in Java and developed at the University of Waikato, New Zealand. It is mostly used for academic purposes and may not work on large data sets.

- LIBSVM: is used for Support Vector Machined

- Vowpal Wabbit

- Knime

- RapidMiner

- Spark

SOFTWARE ENGINEERING

That software must be engineered and not just crafted, was the thought that led to the software engineering discipline, in the wake of a 1968 NATO conference on Software Engineering. IEEE Computer Society published '*the Guide to the Software Engineering Body of Knowledge Version 3.0*' in 2014.

As pointed out by Rick Kazman in the article 'Software Engineering' (Computing Edge, IEEE, December 2017), today we must manage highly complex systems and software. Today's cars are powered by software containing tens of millions of lines of code. A typical Linux distribution has hundreds of millions of lines of code. Software changes are also required to be made rapidly.

'Amazon deploys code every 11.7 seconds. Etsy, the online gift store does over 50 deployments per day. Facebook updates its code at least twice a day'. Such complexity of systems makes software engineering important.

Structured Systems Analysis & Design (SSAD)

For development of information systems, the systems approach helped in the development of software engineering and the structured systems analysis and design (SSAD) methodology popularized by Carnegie Mellon University in the 1970s. Systems analysis and design phases of software development consider business processes and applications. The systems analyst documents the information flow, data storage and data elements, the inputs and outputs to the processes and the external entities or stakeholders that interact with the system. The system or solution architects design the system following architectural frameworks such as Zachman or TOGAF (The Open Group Architectural Framework).

Traditionally systems analysis has used the waterfall model with independent phases of business analysis, design, coding, testing, systems implementation and operations or maintenance. Business requirements are captured by Business Analysts in the plan phase. Solution Architects are engaged to design the solution and the system as per the requirements defined in the requirements document. This is followed by the coding phase when computer programmers or developers code and test their software code.

After the software code and modules are fully tested in unit testing, system testing, and integration testing, Quality

Analysts approve the software code to be deployed in production. System and network engineers get the systems and networks configured and tested for production deployment.

After the software goes into production, operational aspects and issues are tracked by production engineers through service tickets and service management software.

In brief this is the plan, build and run phases of automated business systems. Business and IT Management are involved in the evaluation and monitoring aspect of systems in their plan, build and run stages. Project Management approaches are used for effective roll-out of systems through the plan, build and production roll-out phases.

The COBIT framework (developed by ISACA and IT Governance Institute) details the various IT processes concerned with the plan, build/acquire, run, and monitoring aspects of information systems. These would ensure that IT processes are aligned with business objectives. There must be adequate controls that can be audited for effectiveness by Information Systems Auditors (CISAs).

Agile Methodology

In 2001, fresh thinking on the heavy-weight, document-based and slow software development approaches, led to the Agile Manifesto and Agile Alliance. The best features of the methodologies such as Extreme Programming (XP), Scrum, the Dynamic Systems Development Model (DSDM), Adaptive Software Development, Crystal,

Feature-Driven Development, and Pragmatic Programming, were incorporated into the Agile methodology. Agile approach can focus on the business processes to build what is right for business, and the approach can focus on the software technologies. The technology oriented agile approach focuses on simple designs, continuous testing and feedback, and system integration.

The Agile approach focused more on teams than on the hierarchical and segregated roles in development project teams. Software teams became flat organizations. 'Craftsmanship over crap' was emphasized. Today the agile methodology and dev-ops approach that followed, are preferred to the waterfall model and similar approaches.

DevOps approach

DevOps approach was an extension of the agile methodology, with the focus on bridging business and customers.

Effective management of technology is critical for business competitiveness, as pointed out by the DevOps evangelists Kim Gene, Jez Humble, Patrick Debois, John Willis, Kevin Behr, and George Stafford. Agility, Reliability, and Security are the key factors that led to the emergence and adoption of DevOps methodology for software development.

DevOps methodology involves an iterative and fast systems development approach going back and forth between business requirements and operational aspects of implementation. The important point to remember is to align technological requirements with business objectives. It is also necessary to consider operational challenges in implementing and maintaining the applications and data. DevOps implementation must cover all the connected systems, networks and communication systems. Identity and access control and management must also be considered. Security must be baked into DevOps. The DevSecOps approach has been proposed to incorporate security into DevOps methodology.

Kim, Behr & Spafford (2017) in their novel *'The Phoenix Project'* describe how in the hypothetical firm *Parts Unlimited,* Business and IT pull together to finish the hypothetical *Phoenix Project* that had budget and time overruns. Bill, the IT Manager was able to fix the mess in 90 days by leveraging DevOps.

The Three Ways philosophy of DevOps is expounded in the novel. These are:

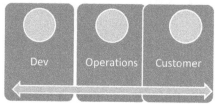

First, the left-to-right work flow from development to IT Operations and then to the customer is considered. The workflow is optimized using small batches and intervals of work, looking at defects and quality and keeping the overarching global goals in mind. Keeping the teams small to five to ten members (in line with 'Amazon's two pizza rule (2PT) or having teams just large enough to be fed by two pizzas) will help better communication and productivity.

The Second Way considers constant feedback from right

to left, helping to identify and prevent problems, and remediating issues and problems as they arise. The deployment pipeline is constantly monitored to make corrective actions at the build and test phases.

The Third Way fosters a culture of continual experimentation (innovation) and risk taking. When things go wrong, the team retreats to Plan B-- a place of safety to resume operations. The innovative teams work in an atmosphere of high trust and collaboration as against a toxic culture fostering fear, order taking, low trust and command-and-control. The Third Way is based on the Toyota Kata practice that is incorporated in the 'Plan, Do, Check, Act' cycle. Toyota Kata practice requires a two-week improvement cycle requiring a supervisor to improve something every two weeks.

As pointed out by the authors, DevOps does not replace ITIL (IT Infrastructure Library) or ITSM (IT Service Management) framework and standards that focus on service design and delivery and on incident and problem management. DevOps is compatible with the Agile Development methodology and is in tune with ITIL / ITSM standards.

The novel 'Phoenix Project' is like Dr. Eliyahu Goldratt's seminal book, 'The Goal: A Process of Ongoing Improvement' in which Dr. Goldratt explained the 'lean' philosophy, identifying various constraints and bottlenecks that escalate costs and delivery schedules in a manufacturing plant.

Kim, Humble, DeBois & Willis (2016) have explained the DevOps approach further in their book 'The DevOps

Handbook – How to Create World-Class Agility, Reliability, & Security in Technology Organizations'. The DevOps approach helps to integrate Product Management, Development, QA, IT Operations, and Information Security, leading to effective management of technology.

Architectural Approach

Architectural approaches are well explained in the Zachman Framework, The Open Group (TOGAF) architectural framework and the SABSA framework. SABSA focuses more on security architecture.

The underlying concept of all these approaches is that technology must be aligned to business objectives, that technology implementation must have a top-down approach starting from the overarching business objectives, business processes and then driving down to the application and technology components covering systems, networks, databases and code that will support the applications that automate the business processes. A detailed framework will answer the why, what, how, where, when, and who of the system that is built. The operations layer will help to tie all components together and may use the ITIL (IT Infrastructure Library) components for better service delivery.

Monolith vs. Micro-Services Architecture

As mentioned by Gene, et al. (2016) in their book 'The DevOps Handbook', tightly-coupled monolithic architectures defined major applications such as eBay's C++ application, Amazon's OBIDOS, or Twitter's Rails front-end, or LinkedIn's Leo. They had all functionality in one application, making scaling difficult and leading to long build times.

3 tier applications separated into presentation, application, and database layers were also monolithic.

Micro-services architecture has resolved many of the issues of monolithic applications. They are modular and independent, have isolated persistence, and have a graph relationship as against the three tiers of separation.

The units are independent and can be tested and deployed independently. In the case of Amazon, the OBIDOS monolith evolved into several service-oriented modules that were distributed and decentralized. By 2015, Amazon was performing 136,000 deployments per day.

The World of APIs & Digital Platforms

The Service Oriented Architecture (SOA) and the micro services architecture that is based on SOA, have promoted the coupling between various modules using APIs (Application Programming Interfaces). APIs have led to development of commercial applications in the cloud to which anyone can hook on, without taking the effort to reinvent the wheel. When posting a message on a social network, reading news on a smart phone, or making purchases online, API calls are made. The digital platform business models (of Amazon, Google, Facebook, Uber, etc.) depend on APIs.

Gartner calls it the API Economy (*From APIs to Ecosystems: API Economy Best Practices for Building a Digital Platform, 13 July 2017*) where APIs hold the key to connecting legacy business applications to digital platforms in the cloud. Enterprises are now forced to use APIs to self-service access points for channel partners, supply chain participants, internal developers, and customers using mobile applications or web applications.

RESTful API

In a connected enterprise with customers and external partners having online access, the prior approach to exposing enterprise data to for external access was by building APIs using web services, XML, and SOAP protocol.

Since mobile and web-based services are widely used now, the REST architecture has emerged as a de facto standard for API integration across systems. RESTful APIs are lightweight and meet the high-performance needs of mobile applications and distributed networks.

The REST (Representational State Transfer) model formulated by Roy Fielding in 2000 is a distributed computing model. Resources connected by APIs are represented as URL and access uses the WEB methods of GET, POST, PUT, and DELETE. REST can consume data streams in multiple formats including HTML, XML, and JSON (Java Script Object Notation). JSON uses JavaScript to describe the data elements involved.

REST is today the lingua franca for mobile computing and is now the default API for online business. REST/JSON is now preferred for database access. We can see SOAP requests declining and REST/JSON requests on the increase in API requests. The ETL (Extract, Transform, and Load) batch processing mode of mapping source and destination data is disappearing as real-time and fast responses are required in online transactions. REST APIs can interface with both SQL and non-SQL databases in real-time.

In mobile computing environments, fast data response is crucial. JavaScript and REST/JSON APIs provide the solution for mobile computing. For database access the ODBC/JDBC fat client architecture is now replaced by REST/JSON requests.

Management of diverse APIs across the enterprise, and across various user communities internal and external, would be challenging. They must integrate with existing applications and middleware. There must be a policy-based framework to control security, access, and runtime attributes to ensure transactional and data integrity, privacy, and availability of systems, applications, and networks.

Design of APIs would require identifying the core IT that runs the business and edge IT requiring integration. Design of API hubs and bridges must be given due importance to build dynamic, agile ecosystems of products, services, and channel partners. (Ed Julson, 'The Role of APIs in the Digital Enterprise', CIO Review).

REST API provides the connectivity platform or interfaces to the resources defined. The JavaScript and JSON logic must be separate from the business logic, also referred to as 'reactive' logic. Reactive programming makes it easier to change as business requirements change. It also facilitates database access and database development incorporating even non-SQL databases.

Can we trust code?

Despite all the testing and quality control, errors creep into the algorithms and the software code itself. Hackers identify and exploit vulnerabilities in the software code, particularly in web applications. SQL injection, cross-site scripting, parameter tampering, run-time malware code injection, etc. are well known attack methods included in the OWASP (Open Web Application Software Project) top 10 web application vulnerabilities. Application code must be scanned by web application scanners such as AppScan, WebInspect, Cenzic, Web Scarab, Fortify, etc. to identify and remediate the vulnerabilities in the code. The algorithms must also be tested to guarantee that they function as desired.

PART III
APPLIED TECH

Robotic Manufacturing

3D Printing

Blockchain

VR/AR/Mixed Reality

Autonomous Vehicles

Drones

Wearables

Food Computing

Chapter 8

THE FUTURE OF MANUFACTURING

Robotics, 3D Printing and additive manufacturing, nanotechnology, and bio-engineering are revolutionizing the world of manufacturing.

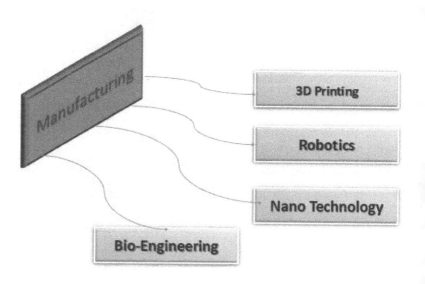

Robotic Manufacturing

Robots are today extensively used in the manufacturing industry and in warehouses. Industrial robots are mostly employed in the automobile industry. Other manufacturing sectors using industrial robots include metal fabrication, food/consumer goods, semiconductors and electronics/photonics, life sciences, pharma and biomedical engineering, plastics and rubber manufacturing. The number of industrial robots world-wide is crossing 2 million in 2017. They are mostly in South Korea, Japan, Germany, USA, and China.

Manufacturing robots trace their origin to the numerically controlled (NC) machines of the late 1930s. General Motors started using an industrial robot in 1961, manufactured by Unimation. In 1969, Victor Scheinman invented the Stanford robotic arm at Stanford University. The robot arm was used in NASA's space missions.

Later, ABB and others introduced robots to assemble small parts and to perform quality control. Robots deployed in manufacturing are huge in size and there are safety issues for humans who get close to their whirling arms. This has led to development of cobots or collaborative robots.

Modern industrial robots are used in the assembly line for handling stressful and repetitive jobs. Joints welded by robots are more precise and consistent. Robots can lift heavy objects, stack boxes onto pallets for shipping, with no complaints of back injuries. Robot arms can plug in the screws, perform soldering of circuit boards, can perform welding or painting jobs more precisely than humans.

New generation industrial robots such as Baxter and Sawyer of Rethink Robotics of Boston, USA, have self-learning capabilities. They can be taught what to do when their arms reach a particular position, such as lifting an object or dropping an object into a box.

Robots are controlled by complex software code controlling their movements. Reprogramming robots is a challenge.

In auto industry they perform heavy lifting, welding, applying glue and painting. SoftWear Automation Inc, an Atlanta startup has developed robots that can sew garments.

Manufacturers of Industrial Robots

Some of the manufacturers of industrial robotic machines are: Fanuc Corp. (Japan) with half a million industrial robots installed worldwide as in 2017, Yaskawa Motoman,ABB, Kawasaki, Nachi, Denso, Kuka, Mitsubishi, Epson, Comau, Foxconn, Staubli, Omron/Adept, Universal Robots AS (Denmark), Hekuma AG (Germany), Rethink Robotics (USA), Robotiq.

Fanuc still leads as the largest industrial robotic manufacturer in the world.

Fanuc R-2000iC industrial robots with pedestal and rack mount versions with payloads designed for material handling and welding operations. LR Mate 200iD mini-robots are deployed for various manufacturing operations including those requiring access into small spaces.

Fanuc's SCARA robots are used in assembly,

testing/inspection, and packaging processes in consumer electronics, auto components, plastics, food and beverage, lab automation, appliances, and medical device manufacturing.

Fanuc robots incorporate integrated iRVision, force sensing, conveyor tracking, fieldbus connectivity, and integrated safety. The Selective Compliance Assembly Robot Arm (SCARA)'s iRProgrammer software interface can be used for programming with tablet computers or PCs and can be accessed via a web browser.

Collaborative robots

Older types of factory robots swing their steel arms with force making it unsafe for humans to be around. New robots are built to be collaborative, and have sonar or cameras to sense when people are nearby so that they can slow down or stop to avoid hurting people.

Baxter from Rethink Robotics is a collaborative robot that can be used for moving materials, picking up parts, and packing or unpacking boxes. The robot's speed will be restricted by safety considerations.

Fanuk's CR-35iA robot is a collaborative robot that can work alongside humans without the need for safety fences. It does heavy lifting that is physically demanding for humans. The seven-axis R-1000iA/120F-7B industrial robot has a payload of 120 kg.

3D Printing and Additive Manufacturing

Manufacturing systems are in for an overhaul with the advent of 3D-Printing in combination with advances in nanotechnology. 3D Printing is ushering in the era of on-demand manufacturing. It will reduce the dependence on warehousing and attendant inventory costs.

With 3D Printing a prototype can be created within 10 to 15 minutes. Even real products with remarkable properties can be created in real time by 3D printers using 3D printing software. 3D printers can create sophisticated designs requiring less material to make and making products lighter.

Some of the possibilities of 3D printing mentioned are: better fuel-efficient cars, new turbine blades, made-to-order cardiac stents created in real-time while the patient is being examined, or digital dentistry applications in real-time. Nano-fabrication is moving down from 10-micron scale to 1000 microns or the mesoscale. This may lead to creation of new sensor technologies for IoT applications, new drug delivery techniques at the cell level, or lab-on-a chip applications.

The Economist magazine (July 1-7, 2017) explores the impact of 3D printers and additive manufacturing on the factories of the future. Just as the Excalibur rose from the enchanted lake, new objects emerge from bowls of liquid resin. False teeth, shoe soles, jewelry, car parts, aircraft parts are already being produced using additive manufacturing or 3D printing process. Expense and performance speed are issues to be dealt with currently for scaling it up for mass production. But according to the Economist, advances in 3D printers will usher in the factories of the future.

3D printing market is expected to rise rapidly. Some of the players already in the field are Carbon 3D, HP, and GE. GE has already invested $1.5 billion in 3D printing, with its Auburn, Alabama plant printing fuel nozzles for the LEAP jet engine, in collaboration with Safran of France.

General Electric founded GE Additive in 2016. GE Additive is now a major investor in 3D printing manufacturers such as Arcam AB and ConceptLaser. Arcam AB is a Swedish company that focuses on electron beam melting systems for 3D printing. Electron Beam Melting can create solid metal parts from metallic powders. It has applications in orthopedics, aerospace, and automotive industries.

ConceptLaser GmbH is now part of GE Additive. Concept Laser's 3D metal printers can produce metallic parts or objects from powders of stainless steel, aluminum, titanium alloys, and precious metals for jewelry making.

Carbon 3D is another dominant player in the field. Joseph DeSimone and co-inventors of Carbon 3D patented a fast 3D printing process called CLIP (Continuous Liquid Interface Production). Their technique harnesses light and oxygen to grow parts from polymer or nanomaterial resins continuously. They developed the technique based on an idea from Terminator 2 where a human rises out of a puddle in real-time. They claim that CLIP technology would make manufacturing process seamless from a CAD drawing design to prototyping (using materials with desired properties), and to final manufacturing.

Carbon 3D printer uses a process known as 'digital-light-synthesis'. It is described as 'a software-controlled chemical reaction to grow parts'. This process is 100 times faster than existing polymer-based printers. It makes obsolete the injection-molding process (forcing molten plastic into a mold) that has been in existence for over 150 years.

Desktop Metal printer technology is another development leading to building and baking metallic parts. Desktop Metal (www.desktopmetal.com), a Massachusetts company founded by MIT Professors and Emanuel Sachs, is focused on 3D metal printing, making it faster, safer, and cheaper than traditional mass manufacturing using laser technology. Google Ventures also has invested in the company. The processes used by Desktop Metal using metallic powders and single jet technology using millions of metallic powder droplets to fuse to form desired shapes and parts, are claimed to be superior to the laser-melted metal printing processes currently used by Boeing and NASA.

Nanotechnologies

Developments in nanotechnologies are giving rise to new materials that are lighter, stronger, adaptive and bio-degradable or recyclable. Graphene is 200 times stronger than steel, million times thinner than human hair, and efficiently conducts heat and electricity. Nano materials such as graphene could fundamentally disrupt manufacturing and infrastructure industries.

3D printing can be used for creating textiles and footwear that can be custom-fit and uniquely tailored to the wearer's measurements.

Customized jewelry can be created using various metals, such as titanium, brass, and bronze.

Applications of Additive Manufacturing

Additive manufacturing provides on-demand on-site manufacturing. Some of the designs that can be created better and more cost-effectively using 3D printing as compared to traditional manufacturing are listed below:

- Personalized objects
    o A customized guitar or musical instrument
    o Toys for children
    o Designer ware clothes
- Healthcare:
    o Medical implants like 3D-printed titanium for replacement bones and implants.
    o Dental repair: 3-D printed replacement teeth
    o Hearing aid using strong cobalt-chrome metal powders
    o Body parts and tissues and organs that can be printed using bio-printers
    o Prosthetic limbs
- Robotics
    o Self-deploying robots such as robotic insects to search disaster zones for signs of life.
- Automotive & Aircraft Industry:

- o Printed drones
- o aircraft parts
- o Car parts
- **Housing-- 3D printed houses**

This field is receiving attention because of the possibility of constructing cheaper and better designed houses in a faster way.

Dr Behrokh Khoshnevis of the University of Southern California is working on 3D printed houses using his technology called Contour Crafting. The technique uses specially designed concrete and gigantic 3D printers. WinSu, a Chinese company has used a similar technique to 3D print houses using recycled industrial waste.

Dr Steven Keating and Dr. Neri Oxman of MIT's Mediated Matter Lab, use self-driven trucks with mounted robotic arms that can be moved around for building 3D printed houses using pre-constructed molds.

What if swarm robots are used as construction workers for 3D printing of houses of the future?

- Space Manufacturing:
  - o Custom-objects created in space in microgravity environments such as the International Space Station.
- Objects of Art:
  - o Art on demand to faithfully reproduce works of art with 3D printing of multiple layers
- **Hotel & Food Industry:**

- o 3D printed lab-grown meat
- o 3D printed pizza

3D Printed Food is already becoming a reality. Since food will be a major issue for long-term space missions, NASA has contracted with Systems and Materials Consultancy in Austin to build 3D food printer for space.

Lab meat is expected to transform the meat industry eliminating the need to slaughter animals. Memphis Meats, in Silicon Valley is producing beef, chicken, and duck directly from animal cells, by combining self-producing cells or bioreactors with oxygen, sugar, and other nutrients. Beyond Meat and Impossible Foods are also working in this area. Impossible Foods produces plant-based burger. Beyond Meat is also producing meat directly from plants.

- Precision Manufacturing
  - o High precision manufacturing such as lab ware, precision measuring pipettes

Chapter 9

DIGITAL BANKING, FIN-TECH AND DIGITAL TRUST

In the wake of the global financial crisis of 2008, financial restructuring and transformation were focused on new

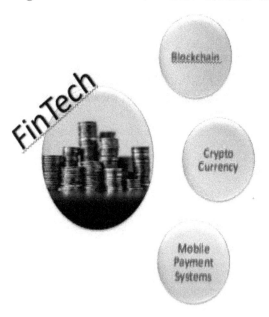

banking and financial services regulations with increased emphasis on use of digital technologies. This spurred the development of financial technology or FinTech. Increased use of online banking, mobile payment systems, use of innovative technologies such as digital currencies, blockchain technology, big data analytics and cloud computing, are indications of the rise of FinTech in the post 2008 era.

While banks and financial services organizations are transitioning from legacy systems to cloud-based secure systems, blockchain technology and crypto currencies are radically changing the scene. Blockchain technology can be applied in many areas where digital trust and transactional integrity can be established without relying on middlemen.

At the same time, mobile banking and mobile payment systems are gaining widespread use in areas of Asia and Africa that are still not touched by conventional banking sector or the Internet.

Digital Trust

"In God we trust. All others, we verify" is often quoted by information security practitioners to remind everyone of the need for security in online transactions. It underlines the importance of trust in cyberspace. Trust involves verifying the digital identity of persons involved, and the integrity of the documents and transactions and contracts between parties.

Online banking and digital payment systems have become routine today in the banking and financial services sector. The PCI/DSS (Payment Credit Card Industry/Data Security Standard) and the widespread adoption of encryption technologies have helped to secure digital banking operations. However, we still have to rely on middlemen such as banks and government to guarantee trust in financial transactions. The main disadvantage is that these are 'centralized' systems that run on aggregated data.

Blockchain Technology

Don Tapscott and Alex Tapscott in their book ' *Blockchain Revolution*' (2016) describe how blockchain technology is changing the financial services industry with far-reaching impact on the world economy. According to them, the internet of information is now being replaced by the internet of value. The distributed platform that enables digital trust can transform the world of business.

The technology currently drives bitcoin and other digital currencies but has ramifications and impact beyond crypto currencies. The technology can facilitate trusted transactions for any asset of value.

Because of its far-reaching implications, the world's biggest financial institutions including Goldman Sachs, JP Morgan Chase, and Credit Suisse, have formed a consortium for adoption of blockchain technology for secure and speedier financial transactions.

Blockchain technologies are changing the way we transact with governments and with each other, wherever contracts and payments or exchange of goods of value are involved. Block Chain technology is ushering in the smart contract ecosystem. Block Chains will help to reduce or eliminate uncertainty in commercial transactions without the need for middlemen such as banks or government. Technology will provide trust in the place of uncertainty, by helping to identify the parties to the transactions, in securing the integrity of transactions, and in creating an unforgeable record of the transactions.

Blockchain technology provides recording and validating the relevant transactions using a distributed database and a distributed peer-to-peer network of independent user nodes. Anyone can check and see the transactions which are encrypted. Privacy is also ensured. The encryption technologies enable block chain technology to provide trust in the digital record or transactions without the need for an intermediate or central authority (such as banks or governments). It guarantees the validity of the record or transactions.

The blockchain technology creates trusted payment and accounting systems, or a 'central ledger', using a cryptographically secure protocol (Public Key Encryption). This allows networked computers to collectively verify a transaction. No single user controls the encrypted 'central ledger' thus eliminating the need for a central banker or a central agency to control contracts or banking systems.

Blockchains can be used for trading value, storing data, or securing systems, and contracts.

Cryptography – the power behind block chain technology

Cryptography is what powers block chain technology. There are two areas of cryptography that are relevant.

1. Public Key Encryption
2. Hashing

Public Key Encryption uses a pair of keys – a public key and a private key to identify the user. The public key is given to the public or to those who want to communicate with the user. The private key or secret key is kept securely by the user.

Public Key-private key pair will be used for digitally signing any transaction.

Hashing is used to create a message digest. If a hashed message is tampered with, it can easily be identified by comparing the embedded hash of the message that is digitally signed and sent, with a fresh hash that is computed on receipt of the message.

Both the encryption techniques—the digital signature using private key-public key pair and the message digest or hash will ensure that the transactions are valid, not tampered with and are from a valid user.

What is a blockchain?

In simple terms, a blockchain is a distributed, shared, and secure database using non-SQL databases such as MongoDB. SQL-based databases may not be useful since documents, messages, and textual information will have to be used as part of data in data blocks.

Block is a digital record of transactions recorded in a ledger format. The distributed database maintains all transactions in a Peer-to-Peer (P2P) network of computers available only to authenticated participants. It validates, records, timestamps, and maintains all transactions in the decentralized network.

The data blocks (or data store) are chained together by linked lists or a binary hash Merkle Tree formed by the hashes of each data block. The digital signatures indicate who owns what, in the globally connected digital world. It eliminates the need to reenter personal information several times, for example to get a driver's license, passport, to record title transactions, paying taxes, etc. Each person is identified by his digital signature that consists of his private key (secret key) and the public key that is distributed. Pseudonymous nature of the Bitcoin network is maintained by not linking the digital signature key of the user to the individual's identifying information such as mobile number or bank account.

A digital fingerprint or one-way hash of the record is created using hash algorithms such as SHA 256 (Secure Hash Algorithm) or Message Digest (MD5). These hashes and the data structure of the block – the linked list---create the chain of blocks. Any manipulation or change to the block will break the chain.

Network of full nodes: A peer-to-peer network of 'full nodes' form the blockchain network. These 'full nodes' or computers are nodes that validate the transactions. They are different from the computers or nodes of users. Each full node will have a complete record of all the transactions in the blockchain. The nodes are distributed all over the world and can be operated by anyone. The blockchain network operators are rewarded for operating the full nodes and for validating the transactions. The Bitcoin network has around 5000 full nodes that are globally distributed.

The Ethereum network that followed the Bitcoin network model uses the traditional blockchain structure, adding a programming language. It also has around 5000 full nodes globally distributed. Ethereum is used to trade Ether (its digital currency), to create smart contracts, and to create decentralized digital autonomous organizations (DAO).

The Factum network incorporates voting for validating the transactions. Factom uses federated nodes and an unlimited number of auditing nodes.

Blockchain transactions

Blockchain transactions involve:

- Record of transactions (with no balance recorded)
- Origination (creation) (the origination and transaction record are cryptographically hashed)
- Digital signature of creator or owner (for authorization of transaction)
- Broadcast of the transaction to the network (a Peer-to-Peer or P2P network is used)
- Validation of the transaction (by a node)
- Propagation or data replication to all nodes
- Verification (by a mining node)
- Confirmation of the transaction

Blockchain software uses conventional computer languages such as C++, JavaScript, or Python. Auditing the transaction would involve auditing the code. Auditing means checking the integrity of the source code, checking the validity and integrity of the transactions, and also checking the process involved from origination to confirmation of the transaction.

Public-Key Cryptographic schemes are used ensure the privacy and security of the blockchain transactions (www.blockchain.info) and for identifying authorized users. Since Public Key- Private Key pairs are used for digital signature, securely storing the private key is important. There were cases of stolen digital wallet (in crypto currencies) where the user was not careful in securing the private key.

Blockchain technology applications for digital trust

Blockchain technology today drives digital currency. Beyond digital currencies, it is going to fundamentally disrupt financial services including stock market trading and capital market operations. Delaware SB 69 regulation in USA allows the use of blockchains to record transactions involving trading of stocks and shares.

Blockchains can be used by industries even outside banking and financial services. It is now being deployed beyond financial transactions to every interaction that involves trust, such as media and entertainment, logistics and supply chain, medicines and patient care, energy trading, government and military applications, land registry, etc.

Some specific use cases are given below:

- Tracking a diamond supply chain

- International money transfers
- Paying artists directly for their work
- Land registry and transfer of ownership
- Record of birth and death
- Electronic voting
- Vehicle registration
- Passports & Visas
- Identity verification
- Digital currencies
- Copyright protection for movies, songs, intellectual property
- Tax payment

Countries such as UK, Singapore, and the United Arab Emirates (UAE) are using blockchain technology for creating new financial instruments and for trusted digital record keeping. The technology is found to reduce overhead costs of record keeping.

In the energy sector, a consortium of energy companies including Shell, BP, and Statoil are developing a blockchain-based energy commodity trading platform. It is expected to streamline and simplify relevant business processes, and relations and connectivity with suppliers and customers. In 2017, Mercuria, a trading house collaborated with the banks ING and Societe Generale on oil trading using blockchain technology. It facilitates cross-border payments, record management, supply chain management, and smart contracts. According to Deloitte, the blockchain is 'a secure system that mitigates risk, increases transparency, provides an audit trail, and speeds up transactions at a significantly reduced cost.'

Blockchains can be used to create secure patient records in a distributed healthcare system.

In November 2016, Barclays Bank completed the world's first blockchain-based global funds transfer transaction that took just hours to complete instead of taking around 20 days as per current processes.

Blockchain technology can be used for many other applications such as birth and death register, property title registration, certifying educational degrees, marriage registration, and even electronic voting. Isle of Man is using the technology for company registration.

David R. Zaharchuk of IBM, writing in Forbes Magazine in January 2017, listed different ways blockchains could help to make governments function more effectively. According to him, financial transaction management, asset management, contract management, and regulatory compliance are four major areas where blockchain technology could be effectively used by governments. Most of the citizen services that are currently paper-based could be radically transformed by using blockchain technology to share data between different systems, facilitating identity management, and transaction validation. In such scenarios, Ethereum and Factom networks described below, are more suitable than Bitcoin-based networks, because Bitcoin works on the principle of pseudonymity.

Nearly 1.5 billion persons around the globe in the underdeveloped and developing world of the African and Asian region, have no legal identity or proof of birth. They are unable to open a bank account, own property, or access government services. Blockchains can help to compile information from multiple data sources to establish and validate a person's identity when traditional sources for proof of identity are not available.

The State of Delaware adopted blockchain technology in 2016 for its record keeping. Thousands of businesses, two thirds of Fortune 500 firms and more than 80 per cent of American IPOs, are incorporated in Delaware.

UK's national land registry is testing blockchains to enable instantaneous change of ownership of property. In Singapore, the central bank is testing use of distributed ledger technology for interbank payments.

Estonia (which became independent in 1991) has built its government on digital technologies. Estonia ID card is a digital ID card that is linked to blockchain technology infrastructure. Major public services like driver's license, passport, credit card, transportation pass, etc. are linked to the digital ID.

Blockchain Protocols

Blockchain algorithms determine the type of data that is entered and processed by the system. Popular blockchain protocols are provided by Bitcoin, Ethereum, Ripple, Hyperledger, and Factom.

Bitcoin is focused on managing the cryptocurrency bitcoin. **Ethereum**, on the other hand, is focused on smart contracts, and in enabling *Decentralized Autonomous Organizations (DAO)* such as government agencies, and organizations to register companies online, or organizing and investing funds via the Ethereum network.

Factom: Network uses federated nodes, in contrast to the 'full nodes' in peer-to-peer distributed networks used by Bitcoin or Ethereum.

Ripple: Ripple blockchain or distributed financial technology enables users to send real-time international payments across its networks. Global markets can meet the demand for fast, low-cost, and on-demand global payment services. It uses a native currency called ripples (XRP).

DigiByte is the blockchain that is used in the online gaming industry.

There are also different types of blockchains: Bitcoin (public network), Ripple (permissioned-networks), Hijro (private network). Permissioned networks are viewable to the public, but participation is controlled by access control mechanisms.

Private Blockchains

Private blockchains or secure private databases can be created using Docker and Ethereum.

What makes blockchain technology attractive is that it is a decentralized system with the public blockchain network acting as a public utility. Risk is minimized with multiple system administrators sharing control of the distributed network and database infrastructure.

Tamper-resistant audit trails enable trust. One can issue and transfer assets without relying on a central authority.

Private blockchains allow developers to test ideas without using cryptocurrency. These can also be used by institutions to maintain the privacy of their transactions. Follow these steps:

- Download the Docker toolbox from www.docker.com/toolbox.
- Download GitHub Desktop http://desktop.github.com/
- Create a GitHub account at www.github.com.
- Download Ethereum Docker from www.github.com/CapGemini-AIE/ethereum-docker

ConsenSys and DAOs for value creation

Consensus Systems (Consensys), launched in 2015 in New York, is a software development company, developing decentralized applications based on the Ethereum platform providing a scripting language to enhance the bitcoin protocol. It has powerful tools to help developers create software services ranging from decentralized games to stock exchanges. It was founded in 2013 by a nineteen-year old Vitalik Buterin, a Canadian of Russian descent, along with Joseph Lubin. ConsenSys is based on the revolutionary concept of decentralized enterprise, building decentralized autonomous organizations (DAO) owned and controlled by value creators, governed by smart contracts. Human intervention is mostly replaced by software agents.

Creating a Smart Contract

Blockchain technology can be used to create 'smart

contracts'. Thunder is a software that is used for creation of smart contracts. A smart contract is a written contract that is translated into code and built as complex if-then statements.

You can create a smart bond or contract using smartcontract website (www.smartcontract.com). You have to enter details such as contract title, description, purpose, can attach documents. You will have to choose the conditions that will trigger the smart contract payment, and digital payment details.

Limitations of blockchains

Security of blockchains is important. Key Management and securing your private key are important areas of security. The validity of the transactional data is to be ensured since once the data is entered into a block, it is difficult to correct it or even remove it.

Quantum computing could break the cryptography protecting the blockchains.

Blockchain operators must continuously look out for malicious nodes, faulty nodes, double spending attacks and compromise of private keys leading to identity theft.

Crypto Currencies

Digital currencies that have been in existence since 2008 are rapidly gaining popularity. As of June 2017, nearly thousand types of digital currencies existed with an aggregate market value of more than $100 billion. The leading ones are Bitcoin with a market share of 46% and

Ethereum with a market share of 23%.

Chinese emperor Kublai Khan is credited with introduction of paper currency in the thirteenth century, in the place of sea shells or gold coins. He found that money had value if people trusted it as payment for exchange of goods and services. There was need for a third party or a trusted authority like the emperor to guarantee its value.

As pointed out by Robert Bryce in *'Smaller, Faster, Lighter, Denser, Cheaper'* (2014), digital currency in the form of wire transfers have been in use for decades now, though the idea of crypto currency is getting more attention now.

In the wake of the global financial crisis of 2008-2009, digital currency emerged as a potential solution for the financial and banking industry worldwide to promote safe and secure financial transactions without engaging intermediaries such as banks and governments. Cryptocurrencies based on the block chain technology are going to change the way we perform financial transactions in the digital world.

Digital currencies provide a cryptographically secure payment system. Hence the name crypto currencies. Crypto currencies are generated by computer programs, while paper currencies (fiat currencies) are issued and guaranteed by governments.

Satoshi Nakamoto (whose identity is still a closely guarded secret) is credited with creation in 2008 of the new electronic cash system that provides peer-to-peer transactions with no trusted third party to mediate. He called his currency system 'bitcoin'. According to him

"What is needed is an electronic payment system based on cryptographic proof instead of trust".

The blockchain technology and the strong encryption based on PKI (Public Key infrastructure) covering the transactions, would provide the algorithmic and cryptographic support to show that crypto currency is reliable and safe.

Because nearly 2.5 billion people in the world have no access to banks, a digital wallet may be their only savior. In the ultimate analysis money provides a medium of exchange and accounting system, for exchange of goods and services. From the Medieval Ages starting with the Medici days of Venice, bankers have acted as middle men for payment of trade. They used paper-based currencies and metallic coins or even shells or goods. Digital currencies are disrupting this system by doing away with the middlemen.

Paul Vigna and Michael J Casey in their book *The Age of Cryptocurrency: How Bitcoin and the Blockchain Are Challenging the Global Economic Order* (2016), indicate how cyber money or crypto currency, such as Bitcoin, is revolutionizing global economy and reinventing the traditional financial systems and structures.

Bitcoins are stored in 'digital wallets' (databases) similar to bank accounts. Anyone with internet access can set up a digital wallet without going to any bank, and use the wallet to buy, receive and send bitcoins.

Though crypto-currency is catching up around the world, the anonymity surrounding crypto-currency mining and the use of bitcoins by the cyber underworld, are some of the areas of concern. China banned Initial Coin Offerings (ICOs) for raising funds by cryptocurrency trading, claiming it amounted to 'illegal public finance' for money laundering. India has initiated steps to regulate crypto currencies bringing them under the control of regulatory agencies such as Securities and Exchange Control Board of India (SEBI) and the Reserve Bank of India (RBI).

Crypto Mining

In the digital gold rush, people invest in equipment and then mine for digital coins. Crypto mining involves digital account keeping using the distributed digital ledger for verifying transactions. Miners get paid for the accounting services. Miners have to maintain the computer hardware, and software including applications and databases such as MongoDB for the blockchain distributed ledger technology.

To mine digital currency such as Litecoins, Dogecoins, or Feathercoins, a free private database or coin wallet would be required. This is a password protected container storing the earning and keeping a network-wide ledger of transactions. Mining software package such as cgminer and stratum can be used. The miner must have membership in an online mining pool, a community of miners, who network their computers for transaction recording and verification.

Membership is also required in an online currency exchange, where virtual coins can be exchanged for conventional cash, and vice versa.

The basic requirement is that there must be reliable full-time internet connection. A dedicated desktop computer would be required. The PC must have an ATI graphic processing unit (GPU) or an ASIC chip that costs from $90 to $3000. Mining is CPU intensive and can generate substantial amount of heat. The hardware must be kept cooled in an air-conditioning environment. Major cryptocurrency mining centers are in China, Mongolia, Venezuela, and Sweden. Availability of cheap electricity is an attraction.

In the current economic environment, crypto-mining requires large-scale investment. On a smaller scale, one can create cryptocurrencies such as Litecoins, Dogecoins, or Feathercoins using mining hardware with an upfront investment of $3000 to $5000.

The alternative to mining is purchasing bitcoins with cash as an investment option. One can buy bitcoins and bitcoin based debit cards from an exchange such as Xapo (xapo.com) in Europe. In USA BitPay provides the same services to accept payments in bitcoins and to get the amount credited to your account in US Dollars, if you like.

Limitations of bitcoins: Currently it takes at least ten minutes or even hours to complete a bitcoin transaction, because of the time involved in validating and confirming a transaction. Glance allows bitcoins to be converted to Glance Dollars, which can then be used for financial transactions using the Glance Pay App. Jamie Dimon of JPMorgan Chase has been the sharpest critic of bitcoins. According to him digital currency is loved by criminals because of its anonymity and is a fraud. He feels that it is money created out of thin air without the support of any government or regulatory agency.

Bitcoin ATMs:

Companies such as BitPay provide a Bitcoin payment processing system. Bitcoin debit cards can be used in ATMs that accept bitcoin transactions. VISA and MasterCard are supporting BitCoin-based debit cards.

Investments in cryptocurrencies

Cryptocurrency market is experiencing exponential growth. According to Coinmarketcap, the cryptocurrency market reached $148 billion as in October 2017. Bitcoin – marketcap was estimated at $73 billion. Bitwise Hold10 Private Index Fund is a cryptocurrency index fund launched by Bitwise Asset Management. The fund captures the top 10 cryptocurrencies.

The main appeal for digital currencies is the convenience and the efficiency of global transactions. Countries such as Estonia, India, Malta, Japan, Russia, and China are considering to launch national cryptocurrencies. SEC feels that this area needs to be fully regulated.

As reported, Goldman Sachs is also considering to join Bitcoin trading. The Bitcoin Economy is now controlled by Coinbase, Xapo, and BitPay

Malicious mining - Cryptojacking threat

When you visit an infected website, your computer, laptop, or mobile device, a malicious JavaScript injected into your browser could be used by hackers to mine cryptocurrency, since cryptocurrency distributed ledger keeping requires high computing power.

The malicious JavaScript on the compromised website takes over or hijacks the device's CPU for crypto mining operations without the knowledge of the user. There may not be a noticeable impact on the computer's performance.

Hackers inject the crypto mining scripts into compromised websites. In September 2017, Coinhive, a company introduced a script to mine the cryptocurrency Monero.

The only indication of such attacks may be a processor load spike after visiting cryptojacked pages.

Malware focusing on stealing cryptocurrency wallets have also surfaced.

Creating your Bitcoin wallet

A Bitcoin wallet address is composed of 32 unique characters. It is used for sending and receiving Bitcoins. Your private key or secret code is used to prove your identity and ownership of the Bitcoins linked to your Bitcoin wallet address.

The Bitcoin wallet needs to be linked to your credit card or bank account. Bitcoin wallets provided by Coinbase (www.coinbase.com) or Xapo (www.circle.com) can be used to create Bitcoin wallets.

The major players in the crypto-currency arena dealing with digital wallets, crypto currency exchanges, crypto-mining, and the countries in which they operate, are listed below:

DIGITAL BANKING, FIN-TECH AND DIGITAL TRUST

Digital Wallets (Databases) are used for sending and receiving Bitcoins and other crypto-currencies:

- Abra (United States)
- Bitcoin.com (St. Kitts & Nevis)
- BitPay (United States)
- BitPesa (Kenya)
- Blockchain.info (UK)
- BTC.com (China)
- Circle (United States)
- Coinbase (United States)
- Coins.ph (Phillipines)
- GoCoin (Isle of Man)
- Jaxx (Canada)
- Luno (Singapore)
- Ripio (Argentina)
- Unocoin (India)
- Xapo (United States)

Exchanges facilitate exchanges of paper-based (fiat) currencies into cryptocurrency and vice versa:

- ANX (Hong Kong)
- Bitex (Argentina)
- bitFlyer (Japan)
- Bitso (Mexico)
- BTCC (China)
- BTER.com (China)
- Coinbase (United States)
- Coins.ph (Phillipines)

- CryptoFacilities (UK)
- Korbit (South Korea)
- Safello (Sweden)
- SFOX (United States)
- ShapeShift (Switzerland)

Miners

- 1Hash (China)
- Bitcoin.com (St. Kitts & Nevis)
- Bitfury (United States)
- Bitmain (China)
- Bixin.com (China)
- Genesis Mining (Hong Kong)
- ViaBTC (China)

Other Services:

- Bitangel.com /Chandler Guo (China)
- BitClub Network (Hong Kong)
- Bloq (United States)
- Civic (United States)
- Decentral (Canada)
- Digital Currency Group (United States)
- Filament (United States)
- Genesis Global Trading (United States)
- Grayscale Investments (United States)
- MONI (Finland)
- OB1 (United States)
- Netki (United States)
- Purse (United States)

- Veem (United States)

Cryptocurrencies in India

In India, the main crypto-currency players are start-ups such as Zebpay, Unocoin, CoinSecure, Searchtrade, Belfrics, and Bitxoxo.

In India, as per provisions of the Securities Contracts (Regulation) Act, 1956, bitcoins are neither 'commodities derivatives' nor 'securities'. This comes in the way of regulation of bitcoins by SEBI or the RBI unless the law is amended. Bitcoin players are considering a self-regulatory organization (SRO) to take care of regulation and concerns such as money laundering, fraud, and misuse, as reported by Ashish Rukhaiyar in his article *'Crypto currencies now under SEBI Lens'* (the Hindu, November 1, 2017).

In USA, Delaware SB 69 regulation allows companies to use cryptocurrencies in e-commerce.

The United States initiated regulation of digital currencies in 2013 by bringing virtual currencies within the ambit of the US Treasury's Financial Crimes Enforcement Network (FinCEN) regulations. Detailed guidelines were issued to cover persons administering, exchanging, or using virtual currencies. The virtual currency exchanges were required to 1) register with FinCEN; 2) have a risk-based know-your-customer (KYC) and anti-money-laundering (AML) program, and 3) to file suspicious activity reports (SAR).

The digital currencies are rapidly evolving. Various issues such as taxation, crowdfunding and initial coin offerings, and related regulatory issues are yet to be sorted out.

Mobile Payment Systems

Crypto currencies such as bitcoin are yet to gain wide acceptance and people are waiting for governments to step in with regulatory controls. In the meantime, mobile payment systems are gaining popularity in countries such as China and in India, and in the African continent. In those countries where cash-based transactions are widely used, cashless money transfers using mobile platforms, are more trustworthy and attractive. PayTM, for example, is popular in India.

In the article *'Will Cash Disappear?'* published in the New York Times of November 14, 2017, Nathaniel Popper, Guilbert Gates and Sarah Almukhtar, opine that in the longer term, electronic payment methods will override cash transactions. Already non-cash payments are popular in Scandinavian Countries, Canada, Britain, Germany, BENELUX, many of the European countries, Australia, the United States, Japan, South Korea, and Iran. In Sweden, 99% of adults make a digital payment. A phone app known as Swish enables instant bank transfers.

Kenya, South Africa, Brazil, Mongolia, Russia, and Chile are catching up. Non-cash payments were only 49% in China, 35% in Mexico, and 22% in India.

In Kenya, the phone company Safaricom created the M-Pesa system, allowing mobile phone payments for customers without even having a bank account. They use SMS communication systems and the mobile app on their mobile phones, to transact mobile payments. M-Pesa was launched in 2007 by Safaricom, a mobile phone provider of Kenya, in collaboration with Vodafone. Customers

225

convert their cash into mobile money for payments.

In China, Alibaba and Tencent are promoting PayPal-like wallets for online payments.

Chase, Walmart, Google, AT&T, Amazon, American Express, MasterCard, and others are now moving onto the mobile payments arena.

Starbucks transacted more than 3 million mobile payment transactions per week (as in 2013) in the USA. Consumers in India, Bangladesh, Pakistan, Japan, China, Canada, Australia, etc. are focusing on mobile payments.

Cash is still king considering its convenience and anonymity. Cryptocurrency may fill that void. A cashless world still cannot be visualized since digital currency transactions may not be possible if the network is down or because of a faulty credit score, or because of non-verification of identity, or denial of transaction for a valid or faulty reason. The fact that digital money is conveniently used by criminals makes it necessary to have security safeguards built into every digital transaction.

Chapter 10

GENERAL APPLICATION AREAS

Every industry and every area of human life are being impacted by emerging digital technologies—transport, healthcare, education, urban life, food and agriculture, entertainment, and our interactions with our environment through virtual or augmented reality, or in social interactions online using social networks.

General Application Areas

- VR/AR/Mixed Reality
- Autonomous Vehicles
- Smart Cities
- Implantables & Wearables
- Education: MOOCs
- Agriculture & Food Computing

Virtual Reality & Augmented Reality (Immersive Computing)

After the smart phone revolution, Virtual reality (VR) and Augmented Reality (AR) may provide a richer user experience and interaction with the physical world and virtual world than even smart phones. Now everywhere we see the sight of particularly young people buried in their smart phones. Soon we may see people wearing VR/AR helmets or using their smart glasses to interact with the 3D world of virtual and augmented reality. Virtual Reality is today provided by head-mounted computers such as Windows 10 MR devices (HoloLens) or Facebook's Oculus Rift. Google Glass projects information on to the eyeglasses of the wearer.

Virtual Reality provides a 3-D visual experience in playing games (such as Pokémon Go) or in watching short movies. In 2014 Facebook acquired VR headset maker Oculus for $3 billion, to provide a VR experience in social interactions, as an extension of the video chat experience provided by FaceTime or Skype.

In the post smartphone world and after **SecondLife**, virtual socializing, is picking up with improvements in VR technology.

In the corporate world, video conferencing and teleconferencing may take new dimensions with VR technologies and private space for social or corporate interactions. HTC's Vive (Rec Room), AltSpace VR, High Fidelity, and Facebook Spaces are becoming popular in this space.

Creating your virtual self or avatar can be fun. Logan Kugler, in the article '*Why Virtual Reality Will Transform a Workplace Near You*' (ACM Communications), details the emerging companies and tools that are changing workplace collaboration and the world of entertainment with virtual reality and augmented technologies.

VR allows users with a VR headset such as Facebook's Oculus Rift to interact and collaborate in a virtual world. This takes audio conferencing and video conferencing one step further. Pokémon Go 3D Game can be controlled using a smart phone. Microsoft HoloLens enables mixed reality entertainment allowing users wearing HoloLens wearable to interact with virtual 3D objects.

Sony's PlayStation VR and Samsung's Gear VR headsets provide a unique entertainment experience for the user.

These technologies are helping the movie industry to create motion picture vision and motion effects.

Augmented Reality (AR)

Augmented Reality has its roots to the 1992 US Air Force project called 'Virtual Fixtures'. It was intended to help surgeons operate remotely helping to see even the location of major arteries. Today the hardware resides in almost every smartphone. Pokémon GO was the first video game using AR. Snapchat Spectacles augment what we see with relevant content.

AR applications can now be downloaded on Android devices such as smartphones. Asus ZenFone AR is a smartphone built specifically for augmented reality. iPhone

8 and iPhone X contain a super-fast Bionic A11 processor with enhanced AR performance. Facebook's AR Studio is a platform for developers for building AR apps for Facebook. It supports 3D rendering, real-time face tracking, object recognition, AR shopping apps and navigation. Google also has its Tango mobile AR platform for AR app developers. With Google Lens powered by AI visual search technologies, if you take a picture of a flow, it will tell you what it is.

Apple's AR Kit is a toolkit for AR developers of iPhone and iPad apps. AR will also become a part of car windscreens and smart glasses.

VR and AR for workplace collaboration

VR and augmented reality applications can be used in the workplace for training workers and professionals. Troubleshooting and remote maintenance are fertile application areas. Surgeons can use VR/AR technologies for better training and practice of surgical operations, helping them to get a more realistic picture of the surgery involved, resulting in less errors and fatalities. Osso VR is one such system.

In the workplace, AltspaceVR application can provide a better collaborative environment going beyond phone and email communications, and audio/video teleconferencing. 3D models over a web browser can provide a more realistic environment to communicate remotely.

Current technologies include:

- VUZIX M 3000 smartglass

- ATHEER AiR Glasses based non NVidia K1 Processor + GPU.
- Platforms : Google Tango camera and sensors.
- VR technology finds promising applications in education with Google's Expeditions AR.
- Daydream (Google) mobile AR/VR applications with standalone headsets from HTC, Lenovo.

Mixed Reality

Microsoft would call its implementation of HoloLens a Mixed Reality incorporating virtual reality and augmented reality. According to Satya Nadella, CEO of Microsoft, as mentioned by him in '*Hit* Refresh', mixed reality will soon be an essential tool in medicine, education, and manufacturing. Satya Nadella described how using his HoloLens he had a virtual excursion that transported him to the Martian surface inspecting the rocks on the surface of the Red Planet. This is where the real physical world and the virtual world blend. He sees the widespread adoption of HoloLens in space exploration.

Industrial Augmented Reality

Google is targeting its Google Glass Enterprise with AR capability for industrial use. GE, Agco, DHL, and Sutter Health are trying out Google Glass. GE Aviation used it on the factory floor.

Lenovo, ODG, and Vuzix are also in the smart glass business with Augmented Reality applications in manufacturing, logistics, oil and gas. These smartglasses with AR use the android platform except for Apple who has launched the ARkit platform. Microsoft already has its

HoloLens.

Vision for the Visually Impaired

OxSight is a startup started by Stephen Hicks, a neuroscientist of University of Oxford and Philip Torr, an Oxford computer-vision scientist. They have developed augmented- reality glasses that enable the visually impaired to see clearly.

Using computer-vision algorithms and cameras, the glasses help those with tunnel vision, color blindness, glaucoma, or visual impairment due to diabetes, to have better vision. It could work on a mobile phone's graphic processor. The vision software and system run on Android.

Virtual World of Simulations

Data is an indicator of the past. To build the future, scientists now turn to the virtual word of simulations. UK firm 'Improbable', guided by its co-founder and CEO Herman Narula, is creating a new virtual world of games with 'artificial or simulated realities' to help us make smarter decisions. Narula's goal is to 'build the Matrix'.

Simulations require tremendous computing power. In March 2016, Improbable came up with a working simulation of the global Internet infrastructure, to test what would happen if the web routing infrastructure was attacked. They built their simulations on SpatialOS used for building games.

Similar simulations can be made of cities, transport networks, utilities, powerlines, mobile phone and Internet systems.

Virtual world simulations are also used as testing grounds for AI. DeepMind's StarCraft, Microsoft's MineCraft and OpenAI's library of AI environments are taking virtual world simulations beyond the realm of decision making to AI environments.

Social Media & Instant Messaging

Use of social media platforms such as Facebook, Twitter, Snapchat, WhatsApp, YouTube (owned by Google), LinkedIn (owned by Microsoft), Instagram (now part of Facebook), Tumblr (owned by Yahoo) etc., is a remarkable phenomenon of this digital age. Social media is almost replacing newspapers, magazines, books, and even the radio and television, in spreading information and news more efficiently and globally in text, audio, or video formats. Most importantly, our digital identities are tied to many of these platforms. A Facebook id and profile or an email-id is what defines an individual today.

Facebook, launched in 2004, is having around 1.5 billion users today. Social media have the power to transform business and individual life. Social media content and ideas spread like viruses. Today the word 'viral' is used to denote the widespread and almost instantaneous spread of online content on social media.

The authors Luckett & Casey, speak about a social organism (similar to a biological cellular structure) and a digital culture that is evolving. Unless healthy content is fed to this social organism that is global, interconnected, and distributed, the unhealthy threats can have a destructive effect on the social organism fed by social media content.

The prospect of social media providing a global environment for collaborative learning, innovation, and co-operation is a remarkable feature of this digital age.

Entertainment

The digital revolution is now rewriting the rules and the business model of the music industry. In a world that has been ruled by recording companies such as Universal, Sony Music, and Capital Records, tech startups such as Kobalt are giving artists, musicians, and song writers their due place and value by giving them ownership of their creations. Musicians do not have to give up their copyright. Radiohead, Moby, and social media star Jacob Whitesides have shown how musicians can find fans and manage their money without relying on recording companies.

Today any artist can launch himself or herself using a YouTube video. Artists can promote themselves using social media such as Facebook, Twitter, or Instagram.

Spotify and Netflix have disrupted the music industry in an astonishing way. Virtual Reality (VR), Augmented Reality (AR), animation, gaming and simulation software, are impacting the entertainment industry in a significant way.

Medicine and Healthcare

Healthcare is one field that will experience the tremors of disruption arising from emerging technologies. Dr. Eric Topol, a cardiologist in his book 'The Creative Destruction of Medicine: How the Digital Revolution Will Create Better

Healthcare' (2012), has supported this view.

Artificial intelligence may create physician robots that may act as consulting physicians, interviewing patients, eliciting symptoms, performing diagnosis, and suggesting treatment options, prescribing diagnostic tests, prescribing drugs, or suggesting surgery. Robotic nurses may replace human nurses and nursing assistants, particularly for the elderly. Robotic surgery is already in place.

Wearables and fitness trackers, such as Apple Watch, will monitor vital health signs and beam them to the hospital and to the primary care physician. Sensors will check a patient's vitals and check medication. The Scanadu Scout, developed by California-based Scanadu, is mentioned by Robert Bryce. The device placed on the forehead of a person provides body temperature, heart rate, blood oxygen level, respiratory rate, blood pressure, stress level, and the electrical activity of the patient's heart. The data can be transmitted wirelessly to the user's smart phone or to a primary care physician. The device is yet to get FDA approval. But it is indicative of the possibilities ahead. The caveat is in protecting personally identifiable information and protected health information in transit and storage.

Instant diagnosis can be made by data analytics computers powered by Artificial Intelligence and deep learning such as IBM Watson. Developments in genomics and data analytics would lead to development of new drugs.

3D printing technology would lead to creation of replaceable human parts. Virtual Reality and Augmented

Reality or Mixed Reality may help to usher in 3D diagnostic imaging systems. Such systems will further help to perform surgeries remotely.

Wireless sensors, smartphones, mobile connectivity, Internet, genomics, social networking, imaging, information systems, computing power, are the main digital technologies that Dr. Eric Topol sees as the drivers that will move medicine from old medicine to new medicine. Genomics and DNA analysis will usher in an era of 'individualized medicine'. These technologies can drastically reduce the cost of healthcare.

Bio-printing

Additive manufacturing applications in the medical industry include manufacturing of dental implants, hearing-aid shells, and orthopedic implants. Bio-printer for printing living tissues is still in the research and development stage.

Wake Forest Institute for Regenerative Medicine in North Carolina have successfully 3Dprinted body parts such as ears, bones, and muscles and have implanted them into animals. Helping to develop blood vessels for blood supply to these parts is still a challenge and is leading to development of 'bio-ink'.

In 2014, a 3D-printed section of vertebra was implanted to replace a cancerous vertebra in the neck of a young patient in Peking University Third Hospital.

With the combination of 3D printing and nanotechnology, it is left to one's imagination as to what the future holds for ushering in of new materials including bio-parts. Building live organs from living cells and stem cells to make them grow into skin, earlobe, or other organs, is an exciting possibility. Companies such as Open Bionics are making low-cost replacement limbs. The Ada bionic hand is a fully-functional open-source bionic hand.

Bio-Technology

Today a human genome can be sequenced in a few hours. Understanding the variations in genes in individuals can help predict and prevent diseases.

Synthetic biology is emerging to help develop even human organs and tissues.

Editing genes of plants and animals can lead to targeted therapies for diseases, and in higher agricultural output.

We may be moving into an era of creating designer beings.

Gene Editing –CRISPR/Cas9 --the power to control evolution

There are around 100 trillion cells in the human body. There are millions of cells even on the tip of one's finger. These cells continuously grow, divide and die. 10 million new cells are created every minute. These cells have the chromosomes. 23 pairs of them handed over to us from our parents.

Each chromosome has genes -- strands of DNAs - Deoxyribo Nucleic Acid (helix like structures with chemical bases A, T, C and G - Adenine, Thymine, Cytosine and Guanine--forming the ladders of the helix.

The backbone of the double helix is formed by phosphates and sugars. There are around 23000 genes in our body controlling the creation and maintenance of proteins that sustain our tissues and organs.

The health of the tissues and organs is controlled by the sequencing of the bases in the genes. When any ordering of the ATCG sequence breaks, then the control and self-defense mechanism or immune system in the body breaks and there is uncontrolled growth of the cells, resulting in a malignant tumor, or what we call cancer.

The human genome is a huge software code consisting of sequences of the basic nucleotides A, T, C, and G. DNA in its double-helix form (Deoxyribo Nucleic Acid) is the code of life. RNA is the DNA's chemical cousin, to control how genetic information is transferred. The genome is the set of chromosomes in a cell. The human genome has approximately 3 billion base pairs (A,T, C, G) of DNA arranged into 46 chromosomes. A pairs with T, and C with G. The information carried by the DNA or genes is stored in the DNA sequence.

A 2013 breakthrough helped DNA researchers to discover CRISPR (Clustered Regularly Interspaced Short Palindromic Repeats)—uniquely repeated sequences of DNA and the discovery of Cas9 gene. It led to development of CRISPR/Cas9 as a gene editing technique. It was discovered from a defense system found naturally in bacteria. The Cas9 enzyme acts like a pair of molecular scissors. A guide molecule takes the Cas9 enzyme to a specific section of the DNA. Later developments of the CRISPR system have allowed the researchers to switch the genes off and on without changing the DNA sequence. The technique is still in the experimental stage.

Soon, CRISPR could help in repairing or altering our genes, even to create 'better' humans. It may help us to find a cure for HIV, genetic diseases, cancers, and even help address the world's food crisis. There may be ethical and societal repercussions of intentionally mutating genes of embryos to create 'better' humans. It may give us the power to control human evolution. But gene editing to control diseases or plant gene editing to help improve agricultural production, are exciting possibilities.

The new technologies may also help us to find cure for many of the diseases that plague us – cancer, diabetes, heart diseases-- to mention a few. IBM Watson was deployed to find patterns in genomic data of patients for over 70 years in over 200 different types of cancer. Genomics, DNA profiling, and bio-engineering, may lead to development of new drugs and deal with the problem of antibiotic-resistant bacteria.

Currently researchers at MIT and Harvard are focusing on gene editing to fix genetic disorders such as blood disorders, neurological disorders, hereditary deafness, and hereditary blindness.

Gene Modified vs. Gene edited Crops

Large agricultural and chemical producers such as Monsanto have tried genetic engineering to create gene modified crops such as herbicide and insect-resistant corn and soybeans. This has been resisted by the public claiming gene-modified crops may not be healthy unlike natural and organic food. Since gene editing is different from gene modification, it can lead to healthier crops. Gene modification leads to insertion of a foreign gene into the plant to create a new trait. Gene editing only tweaks the plant's existing DNA.

Gene editing is cheap and precise. This may lead to new varieties of crops, 'blight-resistant potatoes, tastier tomatoes, drought-tolerant rice, and higher-fiber wheat' as mentioned by David Rotman in the Editorial of MIT Technology Review, January/February 2018.

Transforming Education through MOOCs

The idea of massive open online courses (MOOCs) for the masses is gaining ground. Technology can be leveraged to revolutionize the way we learn. Thanks to the Internet, online education is now possible. Anyone can learn anytime, anywhere with courseware provided online by universities or by anyone. The learning process can be personalized providing convenience and reducing costs, without even going to school or college. A virtual tutor can provide one-on-one classrooms. Many of the universities have online courses and many of the degree or certificate programs are completely offered online. Cornell University has its eCornell web portal. In 2011, about 160,000 students from 190 countries enrolled in a free online course on artificial intelligence taught by two experts at Stanford University.

Khan Academy (www.khanacademy.org) has already implemented this concept, by video-streaming lectures since 2006. Salman Khan, an MIT and Harvard alumnus, founded Khan Academy in 2006, while working as a hedge fund analyst. He believes that a video on the Internet can revolutionize education. According to him, technology makes learning personal and interactive, helping learners to learn anything at their own pace, to experiment, make mistakes, learn from mistakes, and then work towards mastery of the subject. According to him technology can humanize education and the classroom. It does not embarrass the learners. There are no teachers breathing down your neck or asking, 'do you understand?'.

The five leaders in on-line learning, mentioned by Robert Bryce are:

- Coursera (www.coursera.org) founded in 2011 by two Stanford Computer Science Professors, Andrew Ng and Daphne Koller, and is based on Stanford's original online class platform.
- EDX (www.edx.org) founded in 2012 as a venture between MIT and Harvard.
- Khan Academy (www.khanacademy.org): focused on Mathematics, biology, chemistry, physics, finance, and history. Teams with Bank of America to offer financial literacy for adults.
- The Great Courses (www.thegreatcourses.com): Founded in 1990 by Thomas M. Rollins. It is a private, for-profit online academy. Has about 400 courses across 10 subject areas taught by top professors.
- Udacity (www.udacity.com) : Founded in 2011

after the cofounders Sebastian Thrun and Peter Norvig offered their 'Introduction to Artificial Intelligence' course online to anyone for free. Cofounder Mike Sokolsky is a robotics researcher. It is a for profit private company.

Another dimension to technological advances in the educational sphere is the introduction of robotic teachers, as is being experimented in China.

Some of the challenges of online courses are high dropout rates, difficulties in grading, and decreased personal interaction with the teacher.

Agriculture & Healthy Eating

Feeding the growing world population (7.5 billion now) and environmental protection are major challenges for application of emerging technologies. Agriculture will see major changes in the coming years. Drones or Unmanned Aerial Vehicles (UAV) and satellites will be employed for aerial surveying, disaster monitoring, and remote sensing. Use of sensors on a wide scale along with big data analytics will help in soil analysis and crop monitoring. Hydroponics and vertical farming will shift food production to cities. Genetic engineering and gene editing will help to genetically engineer crops.

The food industry is a $5 trillion industry in the United States of America. It encompasses everything connected with food from growing food to storage, transport, USDA inspection, and delivery. In the Internet of Everything (IoE) scenario, sensors will check critical variables like water saturation in fruits and vegetables. Smart packages will use RFID (Radio Frequency ID), NFC (Near Field Communication), Bluetooth, wireless, and satellite communication technologies. There will be real-time monitoring of meat products (for example, checking for salmonella virus). Sweet Green is a company that is already implementing a healthy eating revolution with farm to table operation.

Food Computing – the New Green Revolution

Food scarcity for the rapidly increasing world population is a major issue to be tackled in the future. How can digital technologies improve agriculture and food production in this digital age? A new green revolution is on the horizon with the adoption of robotics, sensors, machine learning, and 'food computers'. MIT Media Lab is promoting what they call Open Agriculture (OpenAg) envisioning the future of urban and rural agriculture around the world.

Productive agriculture has to consider the agriculture product and the various aerial and root variables that will determine the agricultural production. The aerial variables will be the measure of CO_2, temperature, humidity or climatic conditions. The root characteristics to be considered will be mainly the levels of NPK (Nitrogen, Phosphorus, and Potassium), water content, PH levels, and oxygenation levels.

Robotic vision systems and sensors can be used to measure these variables in the food farms. Genetics and genomics will determine the type of product and these will be correlated with the variables mentioned along with parameters of the climatic conditions of the geographical area. An Internet cloud-based program championed by MIT Media Lab aims to revolutionize agriculture and food production globally by providing relevant data to help the farmers to grow their products and to market them.

Hydroponic Cultivation

"Food Computer' or FC plants envisaged by them for an urban densely populated environment, does not require soil. They can be hydroponic, with nutrients injected into the water surrounding the roots. The nutrients can also be 'misted' onto the plant is dangling with open-air roots.

A food product can be developed on a table-top size food computer or can be scaled up to the size of a large container, or a food warehouse.

These technologies along with LED lighting to reduce power consumption are ushering in what is called 'vertical farming'. These are gaining in popularity in US (California, Delaware, New Jersey, Texas, Wyoming, and Massachusetts, to mention a few), Japan, Taiwan, and China.

A greenhouse on the red planet is also envisaged using the hydroponic cultivation approach.

Vertical Farming

In smart cities, vertical farming using hydroponics for growing food indoors, would lead to reduction in use of soil, fertilizer, and water. With increased yield and year-round crops, food availability would be ensured.

Singapore's sustainable city garden is a case in point. The

garden's trees are vertical gardens, fitted with solar panels and rainwater collection tanks.

PART IV
THE FUTURE OF
TECHNOLOGY &
RISKS

Chapter 11

LOOKING INTO THE CRYSTAL BALL

'The most profound technologies are those that disappear' – *Mark Weiser, Computer Pioneer and XEROX PARC Chief Technologist*

What is the future of technology? One of the worst predictions on the future of computers was made by Thomas Watson, President of IBM in 1943, when he said "I think there is a world market for maybe five computers." Admittedly at that time he was referring to the vacuum-tube-powered adding machine that required a whole room space. Similar prediction was made about television that was referred to as an 'idiot box'. Ken Olsen, founder of Digital Equipment Corporation, in 1977 did not find any reason why anyone would want a computer in their home. In 1995, Robert Metcalfe, founder of 3Com, also credited with the invention of the 'Ethernet', had predicted in 1995 that the Internet would collapse in 1996. He literally had to eat his words in 1999.

How do we then predict the future? It was Peter F. Drucker who said, *'The best way to predict the future is to create it'*.

Kelly & Zach Weinersmith in their book *'Soonish- Ten Emerging Technologies That'll Improve and/or Ruin Everything'* (2017) make their preliminary predictions with their characteristic sense of humor, thus:

"We predict that computers will get faster. We predict screens will get higher resolution. We predict gene sequencing will get cheaper. We predict the sky will remain blue, puppies will remain cute, pie will remain tasty, cows will continue to be mooing, and decorative hand towels will continue to make sense only to your mom."

They go on to state that reusable rockets will lower the cost of rocket launches by 30-50% in the next twenty years, cancer diagnosis using blood test will be possible in the next thirty years, and nano-bio-machines will cure most genetic disorders in the next fifty years.

Looking into the crystal ball, new technologies are bound to appear at an exponential rate, and current technologies will become part of normal life or become obsolete rapidly. As discussed earlier, the emerging disruptive technologies of quantum computing, artificial intelligence, IoT, cloud computing, immersive computing, 3D Printing, robotics, big data analytics, brain computing, and others, are going to improve exponentially in the coming decades, helping us to make this a better world, or if we choose—to make it worse and even to destroy humankind.

Quantum computing, artificial intelligence, and machine learning are going to usher in new possibilities. The quantum age will see humans colonizing Mars and the solar system and exploring the universe beyond possibilities that we can imagine now.

Prof Michio Kaku, theoretical physicist and futurist, of City University of New York, has painted a picture of the next century in his book *'Physics of the Future'* (2011). He points to the emergence of a digital world, where computers will be everywhere and nowhere. According to him, after 2020 in the post-silicon era when silicon-based computers will give place to super-cooled quantum computers, quantum computing will rule. Wearable glasses, having full internet capability, or internet-enabled contact lenses, will connect us to the real world, augmenting our vision with data on the objects seen. No one will be able to forget the names of persons we see. All their data will flash on the wearable glass screen. Desktop PCs and notebooks will vanish. Offices and homes will have intelligent wall papers acting as flexible screens. We can say "Mirror, mirror on the wall, tell me more about say, artificial intelligence." Advances in genomics may usher in an age where aging may be controlled, and humans may aim at immortality.

Popular Science Special Edition (2017) on *'Our Future on Mars – Where We'll Be in 2035'*, details the challenges and exciting possibilities of traveling to Mars, living and dying on the red planet, dealing with the perils of radiation, living without an atmosphere, harvesting water and air, farming on Mars, and colonizing Mars. Manned missions to Mars are being planned by Elon Musk's SpaceX. SpaceX is planning to send a robotic mission to Mars in 2020 followed by a human crew mission in 2024. NASA, Jeff Bezos's Blue Origin, Bas Lansdorp and his Mars One, and Boeing-Lockheed Martin partnership, are also in the race to colonize the Moon and Mars and to continue exploring outer space.

Lockheed Martin's ORION spacecraft is being built for deep space probe and Martian travel. NASA is targeting the 2030s for landing humans on the Martian surface. The US NASA Transition Authorization Act of 2017, signed into law on March 21, 2017, mandates that NASA send humans to Mars by 2033. The International Space Station will be used as a test bed for solutions to current mission challenges, in partnership with private space companies.

'**Ubiquitous computing**' was the term coined in 1988 by Mark Weiser, the then chief technologist of Xerox PARC. As mentioned by Bryan Gardiner in '*No Interaction Required – Computers That You Know*' (Popular Science, November/December 2017), Weiser predicted back in 1988, an age of 'calm technology', where technology becomes a part of everyday life and becomes indistinguishable from it.

New technologies will appear only if the enablers are strengthened. Along with technologies and their drivers such as data analytics, and algorithms, organizations must focus on the enablers of new technologies and applications. They are the people, their creativity, and innovative minds, their knowledge and expertise, organizational learning, and the knowledge derived from massive data, driving innovations and better systems.

How Far is Singularity?

Soon, we will see intelligent machines everywhere. The point of singularity where machines will surpass humans in intelligence may not be far away. In fact, machines have shown their superiority in many areas, where human capabilities have limitations. Examples are the DeepBlue and AlphaGo, and robots on the shop floor. We will soon have robots as tellers, nurses, even as physicians, surgeons, and attorneys, or even as advisors on corporate boards.

Ray Kurzweil, futurist, in his book *'The Singularity is Near-When Humans Transcend Biology'* (2005) reminds us that in the twenty-first century, what it means to be human is being enriched and challenged. The human species is breaking the 'shackles of genetic legacy' transcending biological limitations, achieving super intelligence, and longevity, in addition to promoting material progress. Will we usher in a better world, a utopia? Or will it be a dystopian world? What is the future of artificial intelligence?

According to Ray Kurzweil, in the evolutionary timeline, currently humans are in epoch 4 with technology evolving. We are fast moving into epoch 5, involving the merger of technology and human intelligence. In epoch 5, the point of singularity will be reached when biological intelligence cannot be distinguished from the non-biological one. He sees the possibilities of achieving the computational capacity of the human brain and reverse-engineering the software of brain computing, and the overlapping revolutions of genetics, nanotechnology and artificial intelligence, and a panoply of impacts on the social and political fronts. He also examines the vexing question of consciousness and existential risks.

He envisions our evolution to epoch 6 when human

intelligence that will mostly be non-biological will expand and spread through the universe. In that scenario, matter and energy in the universe will be driven by intelligent processes and knowledge.

Dealing with cyberspace risks

Since humans have destructive inclinations and can undo any progress that we make, we cannot ignore the risks that lie ahead, while considering the opportunities that are emerging.

Tapscott warned in 1995 that despite the exciting possibilities of ecommerce, there was also a dark side to the digital economy that was then emerging. This became evident when the dot com bust occurred in 2000. Fred Kaplan in his eye-opening book '*The Dark Territory – The Secret History of Cyber War*' (2016) tracing the history of cyber intrusions, points to the threats and dangers ahead in cyberspace. In 2014, Iran and North Korea hacked into Sony Corporation and Las Vegas Sands Corporation reportedly as part of political retaliation. In 2016, the Russian Federation allegedly was responsible for several cyberattacks. Even IoT devices were not spared in a cyberattack in October 2016 on Dyn DNS.

While leveraging the full potential of the disruptive changes taking place because of the digital revolution and rapid technological advances, we must not lose sight of managing the risks and dangers of this economy and the technologies that drive it.

Integrating security into applications development and

deployment is critical for ensuring secure and reliable operations. It is also important from compliance perspective. A risk-based approach can provide the best outcome

Cybercrimes

Computer-based frauds, cybercrimes such as ransomware attacks and data-breaches have today become widespread. They have huge adverse impact on businesses and organizations including business disruption. These expose organizations and mark them for non-compliance with regulatory requirements. Data breaches lead enterprises to financial losses in the form of fines, law suits, reputational damage, loss of customers, and irreparable damage to business survival.

The question is: how do we take advantage of technology and at the same time avoid risks and losses associated with use of technology.

Digital Identity

An individual's digital identity will be the most important asset for anyone to survive in this digital world. Protecting one's digital identity is a major challenge. With increasing incidents of identity theft, fraud, and privacy violations, it is important to implement digital identity and access management systems and solutions. We have to reemphasize the relevance of Peter Steiner's 1993 cartoon on *The New Yorker* showing one dog talking to another and saying, "On the Internet, nobody knows you're a dog".

Currently at the basic level user-id and passwords are used

for online identification. In financial systems and for online banking, two-factor authentication has become necessary and is mandated by many regulations. Two-factor would involve giving answers against challenge-response scheme or responding with a one-time-password (OTP) or pin sent to a mobile number or email account. Biometric identification using finger-print identification, facial identification (as used in Apple X smartphone), or retinal identification, are additional safeguards.

Public Key encryption (with the public key-private key pair) is used wherever digitally signing a document is required.

With quantum computing emerging, many of these authentication and cryptographic schemes may become obsolete. But it is expected that quantum cryptographic schemes will help to create more secure cryptography. DNA fingerprinting may become the norm to identify an individual in the quantum age.

Privacy

The ever-increasing number of data breaches involving compromise of personally identifiable information, leading to identity theft and frauds, pose a major concern in adoption of digital technologies. Protecting digital identity of individuals, protecting privacy and personally identifiable information (PII) or protected health information (PHI) of individuals or the privacy of their online financial transactions including credit/debit card information, and dealing with cyber incidents of data breaches, are areas that need special attention. Privacy protection is now mandated by privacy regulations. Non-compliance can lead to hefty fines and even imprisonment.

In USA, Privacy regulations such as HIPAA (Health Insurance Portability & Accountability Act) & HITECH (for healthcare information), GLBA (Gramm-Leach Bliley Act) for financial information and PCI/DSS for payment credit card information, have helped to advance protection of protected health information and personally identifiable information including financial information. Massachusetts has made it mandatory for personally identifiable information to be encrypted in storage and transit.

The European Union (EU) has made privacy a fundamental human right. It has introduced the General Data Protection Regulation (GDPR) that is replacing the EU-DPD Data Protection Directive and will be in effect from May 25, 2018. Organizations are required to have a Data Protection Officer to oversee privacy data controllers. In addition to this, data processors must monitor the data transfer mechanism within and outside enterprises.

Outside the EU, strong privacy regulations exist in Canada, Australia and New Zealand.

Specific regulations calling for compliance include the Canadian Anti-Spam Law (CASL), Privacy Regulations in the Asia-Pacific Region, Cybersecurity regulations in the People's Republic of China (PRC), and Australian Privacy Act.

Organizations must develop policies and procedures to protect privacy of personally identifiable information (PII) and protected health information (PHI) and must comply with PCI/DSS regulations for protection of payment card information and transactions. They must have ongoing risk assessment programs and must implement required Privacy Enhancing Technologies (PETS) that may include Data Loss Prevention (DLP) tools.

Safe Computing

The topic of safe computing, particularly concerning children, and teenagers, has received attention in recent times. Several cases, particularly in India, were reported where several students in colleges committed suicide in response to dangerous and suicidal challenges created by video games such as 'Blue Whale'.

Many individuals are falling prey to phishing attacks and resulting online frauds. Corporations are falling victims to 'whaling attacks' or phishing attacks targeted at corporate executives.

Technology Addiction

Technology can be addictive, just like alcohol and drugs. Matt Richetel, New York Times journalist and Pulitzer Prize winner, in his eye-opening book '*A Deadly Wandering*' (2014) drew the digital world's attention to the digital traps ahead. He details the heart-wrenching story of Reggie Shaw, a Utah teenager, who caused a tragic car crash, while texting, resulting in the death of two rocket scientists. He has raised very serious questions that are relevant to the digital age, concerning the relevance and usefulness of technology, the impact technology has on our brains leading to technology obsession and social isolation. Many mobile workers work while driving, feeling the need to stay connected 24x7. Teenagers also find it difficult to wean themselves away from texting.

The question is: how do we strike a balance in the digital culture that is emerging? The answer may lie in a better understanding of the attention and control networks in the brain particularly the anterior cingulate cortex, the dorsolateral prefrontal cortex, and the prefrontal cortex. Focusing, concentration, and mental discipline are areas that may need special attention in the digital age, for youngsters as also for adults. When we ask someone to multitask, we may be inviting disaster, as the brain may become overloaded and may go out of control. As Dr. Watson says in the book '*A Deadly Wandering*', 'everybody has a limit. That is the bottom-line'.

Cyber Security

Security of computing networks, operating systems, applications, and data, must be given due importance.

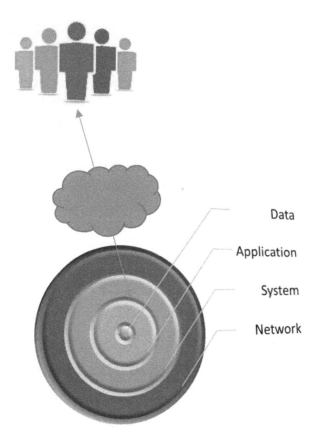

Data

Application

System

Network

Cyber underground is a multi-trillion-dollar industry. Targeted malware attacks, ransomware attacks, banking Trojan attacks, denial of service attacks have all been in the arsenal of the cyber criminals. They are professional computer engineers who take to cybercrime as a profession for huge gains. Identity theft, theft of credit and debit cards, or theft of credentials, are on their daily menu. The stolen credit cards and credentials are offered for sale in the cyber underground networks. Bitcoin and crypto currencies are used for payment of ransom in ransomware attacks.

Cybercriminals easily take over control of computer networks and computer systems by exploiting the vulnerabilities in the networks, operating systems, web applications and databases. The compromised computers are then joined to malicious networks known as bots. The bot networks can be deployed later for launching denial of service attacks targeted at critical infrastructure, specific industry segments, or corporations.

Corporations must have **dedicated information security groups** to identify risks, implement security safeguards and controls at network, system, applications, and data layers. In addition to preventive controls including identity and access management, there must be mechanisms to promptly detect cyber intrusions, and to effectively respond to incidents, and take corrective action. The impact to critical systems and data must be minimized through an effective business continuity plan (BCP) and disaster recovery (DR) program. The DR plans must be tested periodically for their effectiveness. The BCP plan would include a business impact analysis and regular programs for backing up mission-critical data. The NIST Cyber Security Framework is a robust framework to deal with cyber security incidents. It has prevention, detection, incident response, and correction components built into it for implementation. ISO 2700x standards could be a pointer to build a robust information security program in organizations.

Information System Auditors must periodically monitor

the effectiveness of the protective mechanisms (risk-based controls) for mission-critical systems

Dealing with Fake News in the Age of Untruth

Social media is replete with fake news purposely planted by information manipulators or accidently spread by gullible victims. Like the dark web, reportedly, there are business groups in several countries that create and plant fake news on social media. Such news may be targeted at political or ideological opponents. Websites such as snopes.com and factcheck.org, have done a yeoman service to protect social media and internet users from such fake news by debunking myths or falsehood. Michelle Dean in *The Search for Facts in a Post-Fact World'* (Wired, December 2017) has drawn attention to 'the age of untruth' and to the need for fact-check.

Risk Management

Organizations must implement a risk-based cyber security strategy. Risk assessment involves identifying the critical assets to be protected and determining the risk factors such as vulnerabilities of networks, operating systems, applications, and data. Risk assessment involves determining the probabilities of threat actors and threat events exploiting the vulnerabilities identified, and then identifying the potential impact (estimated loss) in terms of financial loss, reputational loss etc. of incidents. The resulting computation of loss can be made qualitatively in terms of high, medium, or low impact, or can even be estimated quantitatively using methodologies such as FAIR methodology. An important area of information security is implementing identity, access control and privilege management systems and technologies, particularly in the context of the vanishing network perimeter.

Ultimately technology and information risk must be articulated in terms of business risk.

Risk assessment must lead to identification of cost-effective preventive, detective, and corrective controls to mitigate the risk.

GRC (Governance, Risk and Compliance) tools such as EMC Archer, Symantec Control Compliance Suite, or IBM OpenPages can be used to monitor risks to critical assets.

Many of the information security / cyber security regulations require an information security program to be developed and implemented in every organization, as part of protective mechanisms for mission-critical information assets.

Cyberwar

It is widely feared that the next global war will be in cyberspace. Cyberdust, Nanobots, robotic armies, and AI systems, will all be part of the next hi-tech global war that has the possibility of destroying humankind.

Today many cyberattacks are state-sponsored. Cyberspace requires protection on a global scale as indicated by the attacks on the nuclear production and uranium enrichment facilities in Iran that used the Stuxnet worm, attacks on Sony Pictures, WannaCry ransomware attacks, Russian-controlled Twitterbots spreading 'fake news', digital vandalism, industrial espionage, and ever increasing attacks on critical infrastructures. Sophisticated hackers can now threaten power grids, online banking, and weapon systems on a massive scale.

Continued terrorist attacks globally raise concerns. E-Terrorists use the Dark Web for propaganda, safely hiding videos, books, and articles in encrypted applications. They also use it for fund-raising or purchasing illegal weapons. The financial operations use bitcoins as bitcoins provide the anonymity. The Tor anonymous network is also used by them.

Stephen Herzog in his article *'Ten Years after the Estonian Cyberattacks- Defense and Adaptation in this Age of Digital Insecurity', (2017)* analyzes the cyberattacks of 2007 on the Baltic state of Estonia. It was a state-sponsored attack by Russian hackers. The DDoS (distributed denial of service) attacks disabled nearly all services used by Estonians and targeted critical infrastructures. It was almost a full-fledged cyber war. In 2007, Estonia was the most tech-savvy country in Europe. 60 per cent of Estonians were daily internet users and 97 per cent of banking was online. The national identification card made it possible to pay taxes and even perform voting online using digital signature. The strained Russia-Estonia relations led to the cyberattacks, virtually bringing Estonia to its knees, as the country was heavily dependent on digital technologies. The attacks led to Estonia adopting a forward-looking cyber security strategy to ensure its digital survival and sovereignty in the face of future attacks.

Cyber Peace Keepers

The question that arises is: Can technology help to detect

and defuse a nuclear missile attack or terrorist cyberattacks? As mentioned by Prof. Walter Dorn of the Royal Military College of Canada in his article *'Cyberpeacekeeping –A New Role for United Nations?'* in Georgetown Journal of International Affairs (Fall-2017), a cyberwar of global proportions is possible, and the United Nations must assume its new role as cyber peacekeepers of the world. Cyber Peace Keepers must investigate major cyberattacks and major hacking events, to identify global cyber criminals, and to prevent escalation of cyberwars. The UN's Office of Information and Communication Technology (OICT) and the United Nations Counter-Terrorism Center, UN's Department of Peacekeeping Operations (DPKO) are already seized of the matter. NATO established in 2008 a NATO Center of Excellence (COE) on Cooperative Cyber Defense based in Talinn, Estonia. The United States established a Cyber Command in 2009. But ultimately cyber policing the world must be the role and responsibility of the United Nations.

With all the nations of the world now connected global commerce, communications, and governance are dependent on the Internet. Any catastrophic attack on the Internet backbone will affect every nation and even life on this planet. Cyberspace is a common resource for humanity and is uncontrolled. It must be protected by an International Agency under the control of the UN.

Technology for Humans

At the organizational level, the focus has to change from just project management to value and impact analysis for technology deployments. As mentioned by Professors

Donald A. Marchand & Joe Peppard in '*Why IT Fumbles Analytics*' (HBR On Point- The Data-Driven Manager, Winter 2017), technical projects should focus less on technology and more on information and knowledge that are produced from the data processed by the automated systems. There must be a radical change to the conventional approach to IT projects that currently focuses only on building and deploying the technology on time, to plan, and within budget, without much considering the value that the implemented systems ultimately provide.

Investments in IT tools and big data initiatives must lead to giving business and organizations high-quality information rapidly to improve managerial decision making and to solve business problems. Businesses must extract value from data and the analytical tools and use the knowledge "to improve the firm's operational and strategic performance." (Marchand and Peppard, 2017).

Technology that provides value will survive. Disruption will continue as long as innovative minds thrive in nurturing environments within or outside organizations. We can imagine the impossible.

Humanized technology

While considering the future of technology, we cannot ignore the digital culture that we are creating and building for the current and future generations of humankind.

Max Tegmark, Professor of Physics at MIT and Director of the Future of Life Institute, in his book '*Life 3.0*' has highlighted the issue of being human in the age of artificial intelligence. AI will affect society in myriad ways and will also impact us as individuals. The focus must be to make AI beneficial to human beings and to society. We cannot rule out an arms race in 'lethal autonomous weapons'. Machines could outsmart humans.

Satya Nadella says, 'It is the people and organizations pushing the boundaries on innovation and applying technology to tackle big challenges that inspire me…technology on its own is just one piece of the puzzle – it's the people and passion behind the technology that bring it to life." (Satya Nadella, *The People and Projects that inspired me in 2017*, LinkedIn, Dec 21, 2017).

He points out the challenge ahead and says, '**Unlock the unimaginable and solve the impossible**'. The impossible includes space elevators, asteroid mining, energy from nuclear fusion, colonies on Mars and the moon or even on Europa, humans connecting with intelligent life (not necessarily biological intelligence) in the universe, and a bio-engineered human. Think of a world using robotic construction workers or farm labor robots. We must also be prepared for a robot workers' union. Zach Weinersmith's cartoon in '*Soonish*' depicts a future judge hearing 'the case of Jones vs. Self-configuring Polyoxymethylene glycol'!

Satya Nadella's vision can be fulfilled only if we merge art and humanities with science and technology. Knowledge will be everywhere at the press of a button and may be provided by machines. But what will differentiate humans from machines will be the imagination, creativity, judgment, and the qualities of the heart and mind combined.

Housing will be a major challenge around the world. Think of a 3D-printed house that can be built in 24 hours and will cost 50% of the current cost. What if we could use a swarm of robots to build these houses to house the refugees displaced from war-torn areas like Syria or Iraq, or to house those whose houses were destroyed by cyclones, hurricanes, or natural disasters around the world?

At the gateway to the quantum age, while focusing on the technologies, we must not lose sight of the immense opportunities that are opening from ideas and solutions emanating from innovative minds. Beyond the horizon, we can see windows of opportunities unfolding to solve hitherto unsolved problems that face humankind -- poverty, disease, war, or climate change. The interplanetary space explorations may help us to understand and utilize human life and the resources on this planet in a better manner. The human spirit is ever trying to expand the limits of human knowledge in every sphere of human activity. The innovative ideas from creative humans are up for grabs by startups, entrepreneurs, and unicorns of the quantum age.

We cannot also forget the fact that technology is a double-edged sword. It can be the surgeon's scalpel or a butcher's knife. Hiroshima and Nagasaki, Auschwitz, and September 2011, are grim reminders of how technology and technological progress can be used to destroy rather than build.

Ultimately the question is whether technology will humanize or dehumanize us. The choice is ours. This book has tried to warn against the dangers that lie ahead—the cyber security risks and the unsafe use of technology or technological addiction. As mentioned, the greater danger is from the cyberwars that are looming on the horizon.

While emerging technologies will usher in human progress and better life in certain pockets of the world, humans have to use these technologies and also intelligent machines to spread out the benefits of technology and improve human lives everywhere, while maintaining planet earth and its ecosystem. The benefits of technology must reach every corner of the globe to benefit human race as one. Technology must lead to better human collaboration. Humans must rise above machines.

In this interconnected world, networked intelligence and consciousness may help to dispel ignorance and prejudices, break down the walls that separate humans from humans, help to build bridges to promote world peace and collaboration everywhere, and help to evolve one humanity. Let this be the dawn of the age of wisdom and better digital collaboration around the world.

As reported by Jaison Palmer in his article *'Entangled Web' (The Economist, The World in 2018),* the first big milestone in quantum computing may be reached in 2018 by Google, IBM or others in the race for quantum supremacy. In 2016, China launched the first quantum-enabled satellite to beam messages securely to the earth and in interplanetary space. In 2018, China plans to build a quantum-signaling network that could launch a global quantum internet. The European Union and USA are close behind in the quantum gold rush.

At least a few of us will be sipping our morning coffee and living on the red planet by 2035, hopefully as wiser humans, in peace and harmony with ourselves, with other creatures, with super-intelligent machines, with nature, with dark matter, dark energy, and with our own universe or with other universes, if any.

Food for Thought

Lewis Carol in *Alice in Wonderland* tells us of the Red Queen's race. Alice was running as fast as she could and still remained where she was.

"Well, in our country," said Alice, still panting a little, "you'd generally get to somewhere else—if you run very fast for a long time, as we've been doing."

"A slow sort of country!" said the Queen. "Now, here, you see, it takes all the running you can do, to keep in the same place. If you want to get somewhere else, you must run at least twice as fast as that."

T.S. Eliot, would remind us in in his poem *"Little Gidding'* that all our exploration will ultimately help us to know ourselves better.

"We shall not cease from exploration

And the end of all our exploring

Will be to arrive where we started

And know the place for the first time."

Welcome to the quantum age and the age of artificial intelligence. Let not Prometheus take back from us humans the fire of the gods that he so graciously gave us.

REFERENCES

Ackoff, R.L., Addison, H.J. & Carey, Andrew . '*Systems Thinking for Curious Managers*'. Devon, UK: Triarchy Press, 2010

Anand, Bharat. *The Content Trap —A Strategist's Guide to Digital Change*. New York: Random House, 2016.

Bryce, Robert. *Smaller, Faster, Lighter, Denser, Cheaper —How Innovation Keeps Proving the Catastrophists Wrong.* New York: PublicAffairs. 2014

CA Technologies. 'Creating REST APIs to Enable Our Connected World', White Paper, January 2016

Christian, Madsbjerg. *Sensemaking —The Power of Humanities in the Age of the Algorithm.* New York: Hachette Books.2017

Davenport, Thomas H & Harris, Jeanne G. *Competing on Analytics--The New Science of Winning.* Boston: Harvard Business Review Press. 2017

Dean, Michelle. 2017. *The Search for Facts in a Post-Fact World'* (Wired, December 2017)

Diamandis, Peter H. & Kotler, Steven. 2012. *'Abundance: The Future is Better Than You Think'.*

Drucker, Peter F. 1992. '*The Age of Discontinuity -- Guidelines to Our Changing Society*'.

Edersheim, Elizabeth Haas. *The Definitive Drucker*. New York: McGrawHill Education. 2017.

Formica, Piero. '*Why Innovators Should Study the Rise & Fall of the Venetian Empire*'. Harvard Business Review, January 17, 2017.

Frans, Johansson. *The Medici Effect- What Elephants & Epidemics Can Teach Us About Innovation*. Boston: Harvard Business Review Press. 2017.

Friedman, Thomas L. *The World is Flat. A Brief History of the Twenty-First Century*. New York: Farrar, Straus and Giroux. 2015.

Gallagher, Leigh. *The Airbnb Story- How three ordinary guys disrupted an industry, made billions... and created plenty of controversy*. Boston: Houghton Mifflin Harcourt. 2017.

Gallaway, Scott. '*The Four- The Hidden DNA of Amazon, Apple, Facebook, and Google*". New York: Portfolio/Penguin. 2017.

Gardiner, Bryan. '*No Interaction Required – Computers That You Know*' (Popular Science, November/December 2017)

Geron, Aurelien. *Hands-On Machine Learning With Scikit-Learn & Tensor Flow – Concepts, Tools, and Techniques to Build Intelligent Systems*. Sebastopol, CA: O'Reilly Media Inc. 2017.

Gershgorn, Dave. *Japanese while-collar workers are already being replaced by artificial intelligence.* Quartz. January 02, 2017.

Gribbin, John. '*Computing with Quantum Cats- From Colossus to Qubits*'

Halpern, Paul. *The Quantum Labyrinth—How Richard Feynman and John Wheeler Revolutionized Time and Reality.* New York: Basic Books. 2017.

How It Works Annual 2017 (Vol. 8).

https://www.postscapes.com/what-exactly-is-the-internet-of-things-infographic/
ISACA. *Security, Audit And Control Features SAP R/3*' 2 Ed. 2006.

Ismail, Salim; Malone, Michael S & Geest,Yuri Van. *Exponential Organizations —Why new organizations are ten times better, faster, and cheaper than yours (and what to do about it)'.* New York: Diversion Books, 2014.

Kaku, Michio. *Physics of the Future.* New York: Anchor Books. 2011.

Kasparov, Garry. 2017. '*Deep Thinking —Where Machine Intelligence Ends and Human Creativity Begins*'

Kim, Gene; Behr, Kevin & Spafford, George. *The Phoenix Project - A Novel About IT, DevOps, and Helping Your Business Win.* Portland, OR: IT Revolution Press. 2013.

Kim, Gene; Humble, Jez; Debois, Patrick & Willis, John. *The DevOps Handbook — How to Create World-Class Agility, Reliability, & Security in Technology Organizations.* Portland, OR: IT Revolution Press. 2016.

Kugler, Logan . *'Why Virtual Reality Will Transform a Workplace Near You'*

Kurzweil, Ray. *'The Singularity is Near-When Humans Transcend Biology'*. New York: Penguin Books, 2005

Liker, Jeffrey K. *The Toyota Way-14 Management Principles from the World's Greatest Manufacturer.* New York: McGraw-Hill. 2004.

Luckett, Oliver & Casey, Michael J. *'The Social Organism- A Radical Understanding of Social Media to Transform Your Business and Life'*. New York: Hachette Books, 2016.

Mayer-Schonberger, Viktor. & Cukier, Kenneth, *'Big Data'*.

McAfee, Andrew. Brynjolfsson, Erick. *Machine | Platform |Crowd - Harnessing Our Digital Future.* New York: W.W. Norton & Company, 2017.

McKinsey Global Institute (MGI), *China's Digital Economy-A Leading Global Force,* August 2017.

Metz, Rachel . 2017. *'Virtual Reality's Missing Element: Other People'*, MIT Technology Review, Vol. 120 No. 4 July/August 2017.

MIT's Food Computer: The Future of Agriculture http://spectrum.ieee.org/computing/embedded-systems/mits-food-computer-the-future-of-urban-agriculture)

MuleSoft. *Connectivity Benchmark Report -Digital Transformation in Today's Enterprise.* January 2017

Nadella, Satya. *Hit Refresh – The Quest to Rediscover Microsoft's*

REFERENCES

Soul and Imagine a Better Future for Everyone. New York: HarperCollins Publishers. 2017.

Nadella, Satya. '*The People and Projects That Inspired me in 2017*', Linkedin, Dec 21, 2017

Nicolelis, Miguel. '*Beyond Boundaries: The New Neuroscience of Connecting Brains with Machines and How It Will Change Our lives*'. 2011.

O'Neil, Cathy. *Weapons of Math Destruction.* 2017.

Parker, Geoffrey G., Van Alstyne, Marshall W. & Choudary, Sangeet, Paul. *Platform Revolution.* New York: W. W. Norton & Company. 2016.

Ransbotham, Sam & Kiron, David. '*Analytics As A Source of Business Innovation*' (MIT Sloan Management Review, February 28, 2017.

Raza, Syed Taznim. '*3D Printing in the Medical Field*'

Richtel, Matt. *A Deadly Wandering—A Mystery, A Landmark Investigation, and the Astonishing Science of Attention in the Digital Age.* New York: William Morrow. 2014.

Ross, Alec. '*The Industries of the Future*'. New York: Simon & Schuster Paperbacks, 2016.

Schwab, Klaus. *The Fourth Industrial Revolution.* New York: Crown Business. New York: Crown Business, 2016

Scott, Harley. The Fuzzy and the Techie-- Why the Liberal Arts Will Rule the Digital World. New York: Houghton Mifflin Harcourt, 2017.

Sloman, Steven & Fernbach, Philip. *The Knowledge Illusion.* New York: Riverhead Books. 2017.

Stone, Brad. *Everything Store—Jeff Bezos and the Age of Amazon.* New York: Little Brown & Company, 2013.

Sullivan, Josh. & Zutavern, Angela. *The Mathematical Corporation – Where Machine Intelligence + Human Ingenuity Achieve the Impossible.* New York: PublicAffairs. 2017.

Susskind, Richard & Susskind, Daniel. 2016. *Technology Will Replace Many Doctors, Lawyers, and Other Professionals.* Harvard Business Review, October 11, 2016.

Tapscott, Don. *The Digital Economy.* 1995.

Tapscott, Don & Tapscott, Alex. *Blockchain Revolution – How the Technology Behind Bitcoin is Changing Money, Business, and the World.* Portfolio/Penguin, 2016.

Tegmark, Max. *Life 3.0 – Being Human in the Age of Artificial Intelligence.* New York: Alfred A. Knopf. 2017.

Tett, Gillian. *The Silo Effect.* Simon & Schuster., 2015.

The Wired World in 2018.

Vance, Ashlee. *Elon Musk – Tesla, SpaceX, and the Quest for a Fantastic Future.* New York: HarpetCollins Publishers. 2015.

Vigna, Paul & Casey, Michael J. *'The Age of Cryptocurrency: How Bitcoin and the Blockchain Are Challenging the Global Economic Order'*

REFERENCES

Weinersmth, Kelly & Weinersmith, Zach. *Soonish*. New York: Penguin Press. 2017.

Wilson, Edward O. *The Origins of Creativity*. New York: LiveRight Publishing. 2017.

ACKNOWLEDGMENTS

I would like to acknowledge the authors and the books referenced in this book. If I have left out anyone, it is not intentional. I have immensely benefited from all these works.

But for Barnes & Noble, Amazon.com, and Google Books, I would not have been able to read these books.

I am indebted to the Professors and management classes I attended in the MBA Program of Ashland University, Ohio, and the Professors of the Doctoral Courses in Computer Information Systems that I attended at Nova Southeastern University (NSU), Fort Lauderdale, Florida. I also have to mention Don Bosco/Sacred Heart Matriculation School, and St. Berchmans College, Changanacherry (Kerala, India), the institutions that shaped me in my formative years.

I have to particularly thank Dr. K.Subramanian, formerly Additional Director General of the National Informatics Centre, N.Delhi, who was mainly responsible for encouraging me to pursue management studies while honing up my IT skills. He also initiated me into Technology Management fields. G. Sudeswaran, then Technical Director of NIC, and many of my bosses and colleagues in CBI encouraged and supported me in my forays into information technology while working as a white-collar crime investigator.

I also have to thank my wife Teresa who has been putting

ACKNOWLEDGMENTS

up with my idiosyncrasies since 1978. My children Thejus and Eliza have also borne the brunt of my workaholic life that left them to fend for themselves. Betty, as a part of our family, has also been our support. Above all, my gratitude to my parents who gave me life.

I would like to thank Dr. John Puthenveetil, an economist and investment expert (educated at Yale University and Wharton School of Business) for his continuous guidance and inspiration and valuable suggestions. I am also indebted to Rev. Dr. P.T. Joseph, formerly Prof of XLRI and Director of XIM, and currently Director of Marian International Institute of Management (MIIM), Kuttikanam (Kerala, India), and also of Amaljyothi College of Engineering, for his valuable suggestions and feedback. He is also the author of the book 'E-Commerce, An Indian Perspective' (published by Prentice Hall of India, 2015). Thanks also to Teresa, Thejus and Eliza for reviewing the manuscript and for their constructive criticism and feedback.

GATEWAY TO THE QUANTUM AGE

ABOUT THE AUTHOR

Joseph Ponnoly is a Technology and Management Consultant and Researcher, and also a Risk Management and Cybersecurity professional. He is a techie and a 'fuzzie' (generalist) with diverse experience and unique perspectives. He has been working for various MNCs in technology, banking and financial services, healthcare, and manufacturing in USA since 2000. He runs his own consulting company *Cinfodens Consulting*. Earlier he served Central Bureau of Investigation (CBI) India as a white-collar crime investigating officer and doubled as a technology professional and techno-manager. He helped to pioneer computer aided investigations in India in the 1980s. He played a major role in computerization of CBI as Officer on Special Duty (Computers) in the 1990s. He also played a significant role in pioneering cybercrime investigations, cyber forensics, and IT training in India during that period. He was a member of the two-member team that represented India at the 2nd International Conference on Computer Crimes held by Interpol in Lyon, France, in May 1996.

He earned MSc in Physics-Electronics (Kerala, India), MS in Computer Information Systems (Nova Southeastern University, FL, USA) (dropped out of the Ph.D. program at the dissertation stage), and earned MBA in Finance & Investments (Ashland University, OH, USA), and also holds professional certifications in information security and management (CISSP, CISM), information systems audit (CISA), and IT Governance (CGEIT). He is a professional member of (ISC)2, ISSA, ISACA, IEEE and ACM. He also served as adjunct faculty of CBI Academy Ghaziabad, IMT Ghaziabad, Bankers Staff College N Delhi/NOIDA, and Ashland University, OH. USA. He is also associated with various Engineering and Management Institutes in Kerala (India) as guest faculty.

He is an avid user of social media, particularly Facebook, LinkedIn, and Blogspot. He created and manages the Facebook Groups *Leadership & Management Forum, IT Frontiers, Cybersecurity Trends, The Humanist Group, BookShelf,* among others. His interests include music, photography, traveling, literature, social work, and philosophy.

He can be reached at **jponnoly@cinfodens.com**

Gateway to the Quantum Age

Managing Disruptive Technologies in Globalized Knowledge Economies

This book provides a fairly wide insight into the knowledge-based economy and digital technology landscape of the quantum age, the emerging technologies that disrupt every business, industry, geography, and human life.

- ❖ **Quantum computing, cloud computing, edge computing, mobile and communication technologies,**
- ❖ **The Smart World of connected devices and Internet of Things (IoT), Sensor technologies and IoT networks, Autonomous Vehicles**
- ❖ **Artificial Intelligence, Robotics & Machine Learning, Brain computing**
- ❖ **3D Printing and digital manufacturing**
- ❖ **Digital banking and Fin-Tech driven by block chain technology and crypto currencies**
- ❖ **Virtual Reality, Augmented Reality, Social Media, Healthcare, Wearables, online education MOOCs, food computing**
- ❖ **Big Data Analytics**
- ❖ **Machine Learning Algorithms & The Algorithmic World**

Also points out the challenges of managing technology and the emerging cyberspace risks and threats.

Author: Joseph Ponnoly is a Technology & Management Researcher and Consultant

www.ingramcontent.com/pod-product-compliance
Lightning Source LLC
Chambersburg PA
CBHW031236050326
40690CB00007B/828